Thirty-seven years of research on successful

love and marriage has taught us many things,

but first and foremost –

no love has blossomed or been sustained

without doing the "simple things."

In Marriage

Simple Things Matter

OTHER MARRIAGE AND RELATIONSHIP BOOKS
BY THE AUTHORS

How To Marry The Right Guy

Building A Love That Lasts

Simple Things Matter In Love And Marriage

Golden Anniversaries

BOOK AWARDS EARNED

Eric Hoffer Awards Gold Medal Winner -
Best Self-Help Book of 2014

International Book Awards Finalist -
Best Relationship Book of 2014

Best Books Award Finalist - USA Book News
Women's Issues 2014

Next Generation INDIE Book Awards Finalist -
Best Relationship Book 2014

Nautilus Book Awards Winner - Relationships 2009

Next Generation INDIE Book Gold Medal Awards Winner -
Best Relationship Book 2008

Mom's Choice Gold Medal Winner -
Most Outstanding Relationships and Marriage Book
2008 and 2009 and 2014

FOLLOW THE DOCTORS AT:

www.SimpleThingsMatter.com

In Marriage

Simple

Things

Matter

Dr. Charles D. Schmitz
Dean and Professor Emeritus of Counseling and Family Therapy
University of Missouri-St. Louis

Dr. Elizabeth A. Schmitz
President, Successful Marriage Reflections, LLC

"America's #1 Love and Marriage Experts"

Briarcliff
Publishing

Published by Briarcliff Publishing

This book is the result of over 37 years of research by the authors with successfully married couples in the United States and around the world. The stories and anecdotes in this book are based on their research and in all cases, names and identifying information have been changed except when permission was granted to reveal their actual names.

Library of Congress Cataloging-in-Publication Data

Names: Schmitz, Charles D., 1946-author. | Schmitz, Elizabeth A., 1948-author.

Title: In marriage simple things matter / Dr. Charles D. Schmitz, Dean and Professor Emeritus of Counseling and Family Therapy, University of Missouri-St. Louis, Dr. Elizabeth A. Schmitz, President, Successful Marriage Reflections, LLC; "America's #1 Love and Marriage Experts".

Description: 1st Edition. | Saint Louis: Briarcliff Publishing, [2018]

Identifiers: LCCN 2018020584 (print) | LCCN 2018021102 (ebook) | ISBN 9780980055481 (E-Book) | ISBN 9780980055474 (alk. paper)

Subjects: LCSH: Marriage. | Love. | Man-woman relationships.

Classification: LCC HQ734 (ebook) | LCC HQ734 .S3864 2018 (print) | DDC 306.81—dc23

LC record available at https://lccn.loc.gov/2018020584

Summary: *In Marriage Simple Things Matter* captures the essence of 37 years of interviews with happily married couples throughout the world. The findings demonstrate that no love survives without doing the simple things. The stories and advice provided show couples how to do the simple things necessary for a happy marriage together.

Printed by Walsworth Publishing Company

PRINTED IN THE UNITED STATES OF AMERICA

10 9 8 7 6 5 4 3 2 1

First Edition

W

E DEDICATE THIS BOOK

to the thousands of successfully married couples we have inter-

viewed over these past 37 years and to our own 52 year marriage.

We are especially appreciative of Dr. Gary Krane and Dan Gallo

for their innovative work in the creation of CoupleWise.com.

They took the best parts of traditional counseling and research to

design a seamless interactive technology that offers a unique

guided therapeutic experience to improve couple relationships—

a design to which we fully subscribe. We are proud to share our

work within the context of their model.

About the Authors

*I*N ADDITION TO BEING AMERICA'S NUMBER 1 Love and Marriage Experts and an Internet sensation, Dr. Charles and Dr. Elizabeth Schmitz are the authors of the bestselling, multiple award-winning books, *Building a Love that Lasts*, *How to Marry the Right Guy*, *Simple Things Matter In Love and Marriage*, and the award-winning classic, *Golden Anniversaries*. They have appeared on ABC, CBS, NBC, FOX, NPR, WGN, TBN, two PBS Specials, and radio stations worldwide. Their work is featured on SimpleThingsMatter.com, Fabulously40.com, SelfGrowth.com, YourTango.com, and CoupleWise.com.

With more than 37 years of research experience on relationships and successful marriage on all seven continents of the world, as well as their own 52-year marriage, the Doctors know what makes relationships, love and marriage work. Their distinguished careers include over 70 awards, 11 books and monographs, 1200 published articles and more than 1000 speeches. The Doctors have also produced 30 photo/music videos based upon their world travels interviewing couples.

Dr. Charles D. Schmitz was a highly successful faculty member and administrator in higher education for over 40 years. He received his Ph.D. from the University of Missouri-Columbia. Currently he is Dean Emeritus of the College of Education and Professor Emeritus of Counseling and Family Therapy at the University of Missouri-St. Louis.

Dr. Elizabeth A. Schmitz is president of Successful Marriage Reflections, LLC. She was an award-winning educator for nearly 40 years, and has lectured extensively in college courses in the areas of counseling and leadership. Having received her doctoral degree from the University of Missouri-Columbia, she is an acclaimed researcher and author.

$\mathcal{C}$ontents

"*T*IL DEATH DO US PART*"* are the words couples use in committing their lives to each other. Why do some couples live happily ever after, while others painfully end their marriage in divorce? This is the question we began researching more than 37 years ago.

We continually remind others that the divorce rate in America is 35-40%, not the oft-reported 50%. Still, the divorce rate is too high by any measure. But the news gets worse. Close to two-thirds of those who get remarried get divorced again! And 75% of those who marry for the third time get divorced. And the simple truth is, most all of this suffering and unhappiness could be avoided. Yes, avoided! How, you say? Well, successfully married couples can tell you. They know!

That is why we have committed our lives to increasing the success rate of marriage by sharing what we have learned from decades of research and our own 52 years of marriage—*most marriages are worth saving and can be saved!!*

We have taken a *completely different approach in our research*—we decided that the best way to understand how to make marriage a success is to study *successful marriages.* You cannot learn about success by studying failure. Success is not the absence of failure but rather the joy and beauty of happiness in a successful marriage.

Over the past 37 years, we have gathered more than *18,000 years of collective wisdom* from happily and successfully married couples in the USA and around the world—people of different ages, ethnicities and faiths.

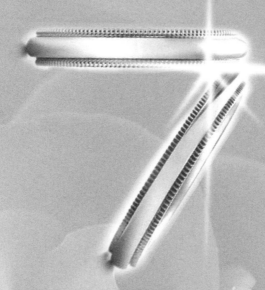

THE SEVEN QUESTIONS

We have learned from our 37 years of marriage research in 56 countries on all seven of the world's continents, that the answers to seven critical questions unlock the secrets to a happy and successful marriage. *In Marriage Simple Things Matter* focuses on the answers to these seven questions:

THE PERFECT WEDDING. NOW WHAT?

WHAT IS LOVE?

WHAT ARE THE BENEFITS OF MARRIAGE?

WHAT ARE THE SIMPLE THINGS THAT MATTER?

WHAT MAKES LOVE LAST?

WHAT ARE THE WARNING SIGNS OF TROUBLE?

HOW CAN MARRIAGE SURVIVE CHALLENGES?

Introduction

*T*HIRTY-SEVEN YEARS OF RESEARCH on successful love and marriage has taught us many things, but first and foremost—no love has blossomed or been sustained without doing the "simple things." Big things don't matter until you and your spouse have mastered the art of doing the simple things day in and day out in your marriage.

All too often in life, people make assumptions about love and marriage that do not stand up under scrutiny—that are not supported by the available evidence. So, what are the facts?

One of the great misconceptions of all time about love and marriage is this—just do the big things and everything will turn out well. And what do the big things include? For starters the list includes "having financial stability in your relationship," "being in love is all that matters," "having a good job and a house in the suburbs," and so it goes. But the truth is, these big things are important, but they are only a by-product of "doing the simple things." Here's what we mean.

If you want your marriage and your relationship to succeed, just do the simple things! Do them day in and day out. When your relationship has mastered the simple things you have a chance to make it work. You have a chance to make it last. If you don't, well, failure becomes an option.

There is another important fact of life when it comes to love and marriage—there will be big challenges to address in your relationship, of that you can be sure. You might have to deal with financial setbacks, serious illness, the loss of a job, or the death of a loved one. And trust us on this—if your relationship with the one you love has mastered the art of doing the simple things day in and day out, the likelihood of your relationship making it through the tough times are multiplied many times over.

So what are these simple things? Here are a few: always showing respect for the one you love; saying I love you many times a day; engaging in simple acts of kindness (breakfast in bed, flowers on non-special occasions; opening doors for them, etc.); giving your lover lots of daily hugs; treating them with courtesy at all times; helping clean up the dinner table; sharing financial decisions with them, and the list goes on. This book, *In Marriage Simple Things Matter,* is filled with examples and tips about how to "just do" the simple things.

The point is, simple things matter and when you practice doing them, they accumulate. Simple acts add up. And always remember, you can't keep turning on then turning off doing the simple things. You have to consistently engage in doing the simple things day in and day out. When you do, you will be surprised at how well this simple notion works.

We hope our little book of essays will help you reap a bountiful harvest of love on your journey of life. But remember this—our book is not a novel that you should read from beginning to end. Rather, we believe you will be better served by picking and choosing those chapters that address matters you and your spouse consider "hot button" issues.

Please check *www.SimpleThingsMatter.com* regularly to find new books, articles, videos and everything you need to discover how to make love last for a lifetime.

❧

A FAIRYTALE WEDDING.
WHAT COMES NEXT?

IN MARRIAGE SIMPLE THINGS MATTER

A Fairytale Wedding!
What Comes Next?

*You've had a fairytale wedding
and now you have a glimpse
of what can come next if only you will
commit to these simple notions.*

*T*HE BRIDE LOOKED GORGEOUS in her beautiful wedding dress, the groom looked handsome and dashing, and the marriage ceremony was a fairy tale that had come true. When she tossed her bouquet of flowers into the crowd after the wedding, a mad scramble ensued to determine who the next lucky bride would be. All was well with the world.

Weddings are so much fun! The memories of such a joyous moment will linger for a lifetime in the minds of most who witnessed it. The photos of the wedding will hang on the wall of their new home, be stored in the photo albums of many, and fill up digital space in their iPhoto collection on their computer hard-drive. For the majority of those getting married, the recall of this significant moment in their lives together will occur frequently and exist in their repertoire of positive reflections "Until death do us part."

Getting married is, however, the easy part for most couples. *Being* married is when the difficult work begins. And all too often, married couples find it difficult to get beyond the wedding in their relationship with each other. When the luster of the fairy tale starts to wear off and the difficult part of making a marriage work begins, many newly married couples flounder—they stumble—and sometimes, they fall. But you know what, this can all be prevented if you just follow the *five simple steps* we have learned from successfully married couples over 37 years of research.

First a few overarching rules of marital engagement:

Rule number one
Knowing what makes marriage work is simple to understand.

Rule number two
You have to just do the simple things required to make marriage work.

Rule number three
Successful marriage is an accumulation of doing the simple things day in and day out of your marriage.

We tell newly married couples to commit these three simple rules to memory and to practice from Day 1 if they expect their marriage to succeed. Successful marriage follows only after these important rules are learned.

Now, you are ready for the five simple steps. Here goes.

1. Commit yourselves after the Honeymoon is over to sit down together and share with each other what you want and expect from your marriage. Lay it all on the table. What are your collective and individual expectations for the marriage? How does each want to be treated by your spouse? Are there housekeeping issues that need to be addressed? What are the democratic values you bring to the marriage? Do you have plans for children and if so, when? What about your individual educational plans? Where do you want to call home now and in the foreseeable future? And the list goes on. The point is, issues like these must be addressed early in the marriage and they must be addressed directly. Questions cannot usually be answered if the questions are not asked. Issues cannot be dealt with if you don't know what the issues are. And the truth is, Step 1 is the necessary first step in building a relationship of communication, give and take, truthfulness, and trust, so necessary to building a lasting love.

2. *It is important early on in a marriage to commit each other to the "core values" you want in your marriage.* For example, successfully married couples are committed to the notion that they always put their spouse first in their relationship with each other. Marriage is not a "me" experience. Marriage is a "we" experience. Putting your needs before that of your partner is not a core value either of you should commit to. Rather, putting each other first lays the foundation upon which your new marriage can build. In addition, committing to caring and unconditional love for each other strengthens the foundation of your marriage. Being mutually responsible, trustworthy, and respectable towards each other adds to the fullness and richness of your relationship. Commitment to these core values will serve your marriage well over the years.

3. *Recognize and accept the fact that good sex is not the heart of your marriage!* This is the hardest lesson to learn after the honeymoon is over and the realities of everyday living in a marital relationship begin to take over. Sex can be a wonderful way to establish intimacy with the one you love. There is no debate about that. But on the other hand, if you set sexual expectations high on your list of things that will make your marriage fulfilling, you will quickly discover that sex alone will not make it so. Your marriage will make it for a whole bunch of reasons, but healthy sex is only one of them. In our book, *Building a Love that Lasts: The Seven*

Surprising Secrets of Successful Marriage, we report many first hand accounts from successfully married couples who report how important intimacy is to a loving marriage. They hug each other often, they kiss, they touch each other while talking, they sit cheek to cheek on the couch while having a conversation, they curl around each other when they sleep or just gaze at the stars, and yes, they have sex from time to time—when it's right for them. Keep sexual intimacy in perspective in your marriage. Commit to that notion from Day 1.

4. Remember this important rule – actions speak louder than words! Early in your marriage you must commit to the simple truth that you will be judged by your actions and deeds, not by your words. When you commit to something with your words, your actions must follow. You cannot just talk about "sharing burdens" —you must actually share burdens. You cannot tell your spouse you love him or her while you treat him or her with disrespect. And, you cannot under any circumstances ignore the *Golden Rule* of life and of love—treat others as you would like them to treat you. In a successful marriage, you more often than not get what you give. Kindness, respect, the sharing of life's burdens, and being a person of integrity will be reciprocated in ways that will add to the richness and fullness of your marriage.

5. And finally, all couples must understand this very simple lesson – your marriage will not always be fair, just, and beautiful! All of the best marriages have gone through tough times. All marriages have their challenges. How you build the foundation of your marriage in the early stages will go a long way towards determining whether your marriage can weather the various storms that lie ahead. Trust us on this – your marriage will be challenged along the way. One of you will lose a job. A family member will get very ill. A child might die. One of you will be transferred to another job location. There will be times when you wonder whether you can make it to the next day of your life. Your marriage will be challenged in ways you never imagined. It happens. Expect it. The good news, all of the most successful marriages have survived the ups and downs, and yours can as well.

All marriages go through seasons—much like the seasons of nature. Marriage is born in the Spring, blossoms over the Summer, grows to maturity in the Fall, and settles in over the Winter. When we find true love, most of us find it for a lifetime. Those marriages and relationships that last over time started with the simple planting of a seed. The seed was nourished over time. Love grown with tender and loving care matures into fully-grown love that can withstand the tests of time.

We have learned a lot about what makes marriages work over these past 37 years. If you heed the advice of all those successfully married couples we have interviewed across the globe, you will have a good chance of making your marriage work—of making it not only survive, but thrive. You've had a perfect wedding and now you have a glimpse of what can come next if only you will commit to these simple notions. Start today.

WHAT IS LOVE?

IN MARRIAGE SIMPLE THINGS MATTER

Understanding True Love

*In the end, to understand true love
you must go with your heart.*

WHAT IS THIS THING CALLED love? Let us count the ways.

There is romantic love, platonic love, erotic love, family love, puppy love, unrequited love, sexual love, virtuous love, and just plain love! Love comes in many forms and varieties. But one thing is certain—people in love know love, feel love, experience love, and practice love.

But what is this thing called love? Through time immemorial people have been trying to define love, understand love, feel love, and practice love. Yet, in the end, most would agree that love is something you feel—you feel in your heart and in your emotions. You can't define it. You can only experience it.

Throughout time, men and women have wondered about love, wrote about love, talked about love, and experienced love. Many have said the obvious—"I can't define love but I know it when I feel it!"

One thing is certain—those who try to define love as something scientific miss the essential points about love. Love is not just chemical, psychological, religious, or physiological. It is all of these! But in the end, love is something you feel. It is something you feel first in your heart and then in your head. Love is compassionate, arousing, uplifting, and it is truly human.

Throughout the millennia, much has been written about love. Paul Frances Webster wrote:

Love is a many splendored thing
It's the April rose that only grows in the early spring

Beautiful, huh? And the poem (later a popular song) illustrates the simplicity of love. Love is something you feel. You can't describe it in ways that give it justice. You can wax on eloquently about its meaning, but in the end it is almost indescribable. But without a doubt, love is a many splendored thing.

The truth about love is the following—true love, real love, and unrequited love cannot be defined. True love can only be felt.

True love is an emotion. True love is a feeling you have for another human being that is different from the love you have ever felt for another human being.

In the end, to understand true love you must go with your heart. Don't make love so complicated. Don't make love indefinable. In the end, understand love by—how you feel in your heart.

In the end, love matters. Go with the flow. Love someone for life. Love someone deeply. Love someone intimately. Love someone for you, and for them. There is nothing like it.

Lessons of Love from Your Dog

Over the years, we have learned much about the essentials of a loving relationship by observing our dog, Louie.

WE ARE PROUD TO TELL you that Louie is truly a Wonder Dog. He is loving, caring, intuitive, intelligent, handsome, and a wonderful friend and companion. Frankly, we love him like a child. And the good news is, he loves us right back! And he loves us unconditionally!

Louie is Golden Retriever. He is a marvelous dog. He is a very beautiful dog. He has been our faithful companion and best friend for eight years. He is everything you could ever want in a best friend. He tells us by his "words" and his actions that he is delighted to see us, that he missed us, and that he loves us. And when we come home from wherever we have been, he shivers, howls a gurgling sound, and wags his tail uncontrollably.

No matter how bad our day, no matter how stressful our work, and no matter how tired we are, just seeing Louie lifts up our spirits, relaxes us, and makes us feel loved. Isn't that amazing? How can a dog have that effect upon us? How can our Wonder Dog, Louie, make us forget all of our cares and woes, lift up our spirits so completely, and make us feel so warm and fuzzy?

Here's the first lesson. Our dog loves us unconditionally. He doesn't love us "If we do something he likes," "If we feed him his food and water," "If we let him sleep with us in bed," "If we comb his fur," or "If we take him to the Vet." He just loves us. He loves us unconditionally. People in the human race should learn this simple lesson.

Secondly, Louie never lies to us. He always tells us the truth. When those soft brown eyes look at you, you melt! There is no equivocation in his eyes. He loves us, plain and simple. Just tell the truth! The eyes know love.

Thirdly, Louie never bites us. Oh, for sure, he might let out a little growl when you try to move him over so you can get in bed, but that is only a warning that he has found his "cozy place" in bed and you are intruding on his space. But bite? Never in a thousand years. He disagrees with us from time to time, but we are his friends, his family, and his supporters. To bite us is so far from his mind that he could never imagine it. And neither could we.

And finally, Louie knows the most important lesson of all – we are his best friends, his family, his trusted associates, and his providers. He can count on us through thick and thin. He can count on us when the chips are down. Louie knows in his heart that we would never let him down, never cheat on him, never hurt him, and never betray him. He loves us unconditionally and we love him just the same.

You can learn a lot about love from a dog. Our Wonder Dog Louie has taught us the loving lessons of life. We are eternally grateful for his love, his trust, and his companionship.

To learn the lessons we have learned from Louie is to have learned the essence of love. Louie has inspired us on to even greater love. We owe the big boy! His example about love is a model we should all follow. Human beings could learn a lot about love from Louie. Thanks, Louie. We love you unconditionally.

Love Is Like Learning to Dance

*It is like watching a pair of ice dancers
gliding through a perfectly executed lift –
they are beautiful skaters individually,
but magnificent when together.*

*I*N OUR AWARD WINNING BOOK,
Building a Love that Lasts, we describe the seven pervasive characteristics present in all successful marriages—and we would dare say, in
all successful and loving relationships between two people. We
often use the notion of "learning to dance" as a way of describing
these relationships. Dance becomes a metaphor for successful love.

You have probably heard the expression, "It takes two to Tango."
When we were in Buenos Aires, Argentina a few of years ago, this
point was really driven home to us as we watched the Tango dancers
perform on the streets. Tango dancing is exotic, breathtaking, sexy,
exhilarating, entertaining, heart-pumping, and just plain fun. But
here is one absolute fact—you cannot do the Tango by yourself! It
does, indeed, take two to Tango.

The characteristics we describe are a pervasive part of who
loving couples are **together** as if describing the steps of a well-
choreographed dance. Successful couples have learned, practiced
and committed these characteristics to memory. It is like watching
a pair of ice dancers gliding through a perfectly executed lift—they
are beautiful skaters individually, but magnificent when together.

On the other hand, failed marriages and failed relationships are like dancing in the dark without knowing the steps. The steps appear to be easy at first, but tragically, divorce statistics tell us that too many married couples never learn to dance. Instead, they stumble and fall until they eventually give up and quit dancing altogether. If they had learned to make the seven characteristics part of the fabric of their marriage, the fabric of their loving relationship, they could have learned the dance of lasting love.

If you want to achieve a lasting love, first learn and understand that the simple things matter in love and marriage. Then accept the commitment to do the simple things everyday of your loving relationship. While it might seem easy at first glance, successful couples describe the hard work it takes to make doing the simple things habitual and pervasive in their relationship.

Learning to dance is fun, but it is also hard work. It takes commitment to perfect the moves. Remember, successful relationships are, more than anything, an accumulation of the simple things. To use the Tango dance as an example, in a holistic sense it is beautiful to watch, but the beauty of the dance is made possible because those doing the dance did the simple things—they learned the steps, and they practiced a lot!

Whether the beat of your loving relationship is a Tango, Salsa, Swing, Waltz, or the Texas Two-Step, when each of these seven characteristics describes your dance together, you will have achieved a successful loving relationship with another person. You will then be well on your way to achieving a long-lasting love like the successful couples we have interviewed over the years who celebrated their Golden Anniversaries together.

Love is like learning to dance. Learn how today. And as a good friend of ours in Texas likes to say, "You meet a lot of nice people when you go dancing!"

Summer Love

*The truth is, if we all had our Summer of Love
there would be no violence, no heartbreak,
no disaffection, no scorn or hate—there would
be only love and peace.*

*T*HERE IS SOMETHING ABOUT
the summer that encourages love. Maybe it's the bright summer
sun. It could be the warm summer breeze. Maybe it's the refreshing
summer water! Perhaps, it is the summer vacation. And isn't baseball played mostly in the summer?

Whatever the cause, it appears that most people fall in love
during the summer and get married during the summer—more
than in any other season of the year. In fact, the research data we
have collected over the years reveals that the months of June, July,
August, and September are the most popular months to get
married. Needless to say, we have often wondered why. Why all this
Summer Love?

Recently, we came upon a statement by Simran Khurana that we
just love. It goes like this: "Summer has always been considered to
be the most romantic of the four seasons. The clear skies, the
blazing sun, the gentle summer breeze, and the lazy afternoons
flavor the season with passion and warm love."

We think Simran has it right. Summer is the most romantic of the four seasons. The seed of love is planted in the spring, and when it is properly nurtured, it will blossom in the summer. Love can be felt in every corner of the world during the warm summer months. Couples just seem to appear everywhere—holding hands, wrapping each other in hugs, exchanging kisses and fondly gazing into each other's eyes. Ah, the Summer of Love—there is nothing like it!

"Love is to the heart what the summer is to the farmer's year—it brings to harvest all the loveliest flowers of the soul." We don't know the source of this quote but we refer to it often when talking about Summer Love. We are particularly captivated by the notion of harvesting "the loveliest flowers of the soul." Here's what we think it means.

When Charley was a child, he always marveled at the bountiful harvest his grandparents, uncles, and aunts were capable of bringing forth in the fall of the year. Wheat was beautiful and golden. The corn was ten feet high! The crops they planted and harvested in the rich bottomlands along the Missouri River were simply amazing. But why, he would often ask? What's so special about this place? Charley quickly learned the answer.

Crops planted in the spring and nourished by the rains grew to gargantuan proportions in the rich soil along the river. And by the end of summer, the crops grew tall, they grew healthy, and they were ripe for the harvest.

Summer Love shares all of these characteristics. Love springs eternal in the spring and is nourished by the rain. But always remember, it grows under the warm sun of summer! Love comes to fruition in the summer. It grows to gargantuan proportions. Summer makes love ripe for the harvest. Summer is the season of love. It is the Summer of Love.

Life is fragile. Life is uncertain. Life is not forever. Love today. Hug someone tonight. In love and life, there is nothing more important than having someone to love, and someone who loves you. Enjoy your Summer of Love.

Being in love—there is nothing like it. There is nothing that can trump it. There is nothing more important in life than finding someone to love—someone to truly love.

The truth is, if we all had our Summer of Love there would be no violence, no heartbreak, no disaffection, no scorn or hate—there would be only love and peace.

Go be in love. There is nothing like it!

Penguins Show Us How to Love

*Penguins may live at the bottom.of
the world, but they can show us all
how to live and love!*

*S*EVERAL YEARS AGO WE
returned from the expedition of our lifetime together—all 52 years
of it. We spent almost two weeks on the continent of Antarctica. For
us, it was the 7th and final continent in our 37-year search for great
marriages around the world.

While we learned much from the couples we interviewed that
live and work in Antarctica, the most important lessons we learned
about love and relationships we just may have learned from the
penguins of Antarctica—particularly the Gentoo, the Adelie, the
Emperor, and the Chinstrap.

The truth is, we discovered over the course of our observations
that penguins and humans have a whole lot in common. In fact, it
is clear to us that penguins and humans share many common and
pervasive characteristics when it comes to love and life. They have
mates—often for a lifetime—love to be around family and friends,
and dearly love and protect their children.

Here are the top fifteen lessons about love and life we learned from the penguins of Antarctica:

1. ***Look out for each other.*** Like humans, penguins live in towns and villages called rookeries because it's easier to protect each other from predators and from the cold weather in groups. And what's really nice—most have a short commute to work finding food!

2. ***Have fun and play a lot.*** Penguins, like humans, love to gather with friends and family to have fun and play. Hanging around with their family gives them particular joy.

3. ***Communicate effectively.*** Penguins talk and chatter a lot to each other, just like humans! Communication is at the heart of their relationships with each other, just as it is with humans.

4. ***Be a responsible adult.*** As they grow older, penguins learn to spread their wings, and even though they will never fly, they grow up for the most part to be responsible and productive adults. Almost all become parents at some point in their life. Sounds like a familiar human story to us.

5. ***Build your support network.*** Sometimes penguins take trips together with their extended family. Like us, penguins know that friends and family are an integral part of their support network.

6. ***Smile a lot.*** Penguins are certainly a happy lot! They rarely get discouraged and almost never give up on their goals. We humans are like that as well.

7. ***Show love to your children.*** Like us, penguins kiss their babies a lot! Their love and affection for their young is always in evidence.

8. **Watch out for danger.** They almost always look left and right before crossing the path! They know the world is full of danger, but you can always count on them to be prudent and careful—for their safety and for the safety of their family and friends. We humans teach our children to look left and right before they cross the street, and we do so at a very early age.

9. **Shout your love to the heavens!** Penguins shout their love for each other by screaming it to the heavens! They are not shy about expressing their love for their mate. Saying "I love you" is just a normal part of their day and they are willing to express their sentiments often. We humans could learn to do a better job of this by observing the penguins!

10. **Keep your body clean.** Penguins love to bath a lot, especially with each other. They will race to get to the water first. Sometimes a refreshing swim makes them jump for joy!

11. **Be faithful to the one you love.** Penguins are monogamous, often having one mate for a lifetime. Death of their life's partner is about the only circumstance that causes them to search for a new mate. Maybe younger humans should pay attention to the penguin's model!

12. **Stop and smell the roses.** Frequently, penguins just stop and admire the view—what we humans would call, "stopping to smell the roses." They often stand together to admire the view from where they live and travel. We humans should do more of this.

13. **Share the parenting responsibilities.** Like humans, penguins share in the nurturing, feeding, and parenting of their children. It is remarkable how penguins demonstrate that birthing, protecting, and raising a child is a shared

responsibility of both the mother and the father. You can count on them to work together to build a comfortable nest for their children.

14. *Express your love often.* Penguins often dance for joy at the sight of someone they love. They sing their love for each other. Penguins are certainly not shy about expressing their love! Like humans in successful relationships, they find that hanging out with their partner is the greatest joy of life.

15. *Argue fairly and don't hold grudges.* Penguins squawk and often times engage in lively discussions and arguments. They get in each other's face, but they usually resolve their differences in a positive fashion. Like human couples penguins argue—there is nothing wrong about that—but they have learned to argue fairly and effectively, almost never holding grudges.

You can certainly learn a lot about love and relationships from the penguins of Antarctica! They may live at the bottom of the world, but in the end, we are all very much alike.

Watch our YouTube video, *The Penguins of Antarctica*, at www.SimpleThingsMatter.com/marriage_around_the_world.html We created this video so you can see our penguin friends in action as they show us all how to live and love! In the end, we discovered that the penguins know the essence of lasting love!

Fully-Grown Love Never Fails

Love is patient, love is kind.
It does not envy, it does not boast, it is not proud
It is not rude, it is not self-seeking.
It is not easily angered, it keeps no record of wrongs.
Love does not delight in evil, but rejoices with the truth.
It always protects, always trusts,
always hopes, always perseveres.
Love never fails. (I Corinthians 13:4-8)

A S WE SIT AT OUR DESK today we are listening to a gentle rain. Spring is only a few days away. You can smell it in the air. You can see it. After several months of winter you look forward to the pretty flowers, the budding trees, and the gentle springing to life of nature. You see it all around you. Hope springs eternal in the Spring and it makes you feel good. It always reminds us of what is truly important in life and in love.

And the birds seem to be looking forward to it as they are frolicking around the backyard trees in search, it seems, of other birds to hang around with. Maybe they are looking for love. They surely will find it today. Spring has sprung!

We have always felt that Spring, in so many ways, is a great metaphor for the evolution of true love. You start with a gentle rain and the seeds of love you planted start to grow until some day the love is real and fully-grown. Nature has a wonderful way of making us reflect on our life, our love, and all the good that surrounds us. Spring reminds us that fully-grown love never fails.

The amazing thing about fully-grown true love is that it adds so much to your life and to the life of the one you love. And interestingly enough we have found the quote from the Bible (I Corinthians 13:4-8) to be awfully apropos as a way of describing all of the successfully married couples we have interviewed over the years. Irrespective of your spiritual persuasion, these words written so long ago still apply today. Successfully married couples engage in fully-grown love and we believe this passage describes such love in all the right ways.

As we have often said, all marriages go through seasons – much like the seasons of nature. It is born in the Spring, blossoms over the Summer, grows to maturity in the Fall, and settles in over the Winter. When we find true love, most of us find it for a lifetime. We find it for the four seasons of life. Those marriages and relationships that last over time started with the simple planting of a seed. The seed was nourished over time. Love grown with tender loving care matures into fully-grown love that can withstand the tests of time.

Enjoy love. Enjoy life. Relish the seasons together.

Love's Essential Virtues

We would offer that gratitude is the secret of a successful loving relationship.

*T*HIS MORNING, A GREAT FRIEND of ours sent along an article that we were really taken with. The article was by Dr. Tom Lickona based upon his book entitled *Character Matters: How to Help our Children Develop Good Judgment, Integrity, and Other Essential Virtues* (Simon & Schuster, ©2004). We were struck by the similarity of the "virtues" he believes essential for "strong character" and the virtues we have discovered in our research over the years about successful loving relationships.

The first essential virtue highlighted by Dr. Lickona is "wisdom." According to Tom, wisdom is the master virtue that directs all others. Wisdom "tells us how to put the other virtues into practice – when to act, how to act, and how to balance different virtues when they conflict" such as "telling the honest truth" even when it "might hurt someone's feelings." We refer to this notion often in our book when we speak of the importance of honesty in our relationships with those we love.

The second virtue is justice according to Dr. Lickona. "Justice means respecting the rights of all persons." In our book, we refer to this virtue as the Golden Rule—do unto others as you would have them do unto you.

The third virtue is "fortitude." According to Lickona, "fortitude enables us to do what is right in the face of difficulty." Or, more succinctly, doing the "hard right instead of the easy wrong." As we discuss in our book, all successful loving relationships have hard times, great challenges, and failures. More importantly, however, those whose love lasts a lifetime have overcome the challenges in life and have been strengthened by them. Overcoming these challenges together makes for a stronger and even more loving relationship. Fortitude is the strength to carry on even when we find it hard in our relationships to see the light at the end of the tunnel.

"Self-Control" is the fourth virtue. In its simplest terms, "self-control is the ability and the strength to govern ourselves—to control our temper and to regulate our appetites and passions." It is as Lickona says, the "power to resist temptation." All marriages and loving relationships have their temptations. Trust us on that. The successful ones don't act on their temptations; hence, they survive and thrive.

The fifth virtue according to Lickona is "love"—"the willingness to sacrifice for the sake of another." Successful loving relationships quickly learn that their relationship is not about "you" or "me." It is about "we" and "us." This is a critical factor in successful relationships. Suffice it to say, people who are truly in love do not spend their time finding fault with each other—they do not spend their time putting down or belittling each other. They find strength in the virtues of each other. They love each other in the truest sense of the word.

As the purveyors of positive love, we really like Lickona's sixth virtue—"positive attitude." We once heard a speaker say, "If you frown, you frown alone, but a smile is infectious!" Maintaining a positive attitude is a great virtue. Who wants to be around negative people? Successful loving relationships work like this as well. If your spouse or your lover is always in a negative mood you will work hard not to be around them. The choice of being negative or positive is ours. Choose positive!

Hard work is the "seventh indispensable virtue" according to Lickona. If you want to be successful in love and life you must work hard. Nothing worth having in a relationship comes easy. You must earn it. Love is something you earn. As we say all the time, the simple things required to make love work take lots of hard work, day in and day out, throughout the life of the loving relationship.

Our favorite virtue is "integrity." As Lickona says, "Integrity is adhering to moral principle, being faithful to moral conscience, keeping your word, and standing up for what we believe." In love and marriage, you don't cheat on the one you love! You don't lie to the one you love. You are faithful to the one you love. There are no exceptions to this basic virtue. To truly love someone is to tell the truth to them and to yourself.

Dr. Lickona reminds us that "Gratitude is often described as the secret of a happy life." We would offer that gratitude is the secret of a successful loving relationship. We must show gratitude for the one we purport to love. We should always take the time to thank those we love for their support, their understanding, their sacrifice for us, and for their love. Always show your gratitude to the one you love. They will love you for it!

And finally, the tenth virtue according to Dr. Lickona is "humility." Humility "makes us aware of our imperfections and leads us to become a better person." And as in love and marriage, "humility enables us to take responsibility for our faults and failings (rather than blaming someone else), apologize for them and seek to make amends." To be truly in love, in our opinion, requires us to recognize that we are not the center of the universe – that the world does not revolve around us. People who are truly in love, learn from each other, they respect each other, they value each other, and they recognize that in the best loving relationships, personal humility allows us to understand the simple notion that trying to prove you are right when you are clearly wrong, is not a virtue. Trying to win a senseless and pointless argument is not a virtue. It is good to be humble!

We would encourage you to read more of Dr. Lickona's work and you will see as we do that his "essential virtues" are, in many ways, a mirror of our "seven secrets of a successful marriage."

Is Love Blind?

Our love is blind. It is love we feel.
It is not love we see

SCIENTISTS AT UNIVERSITY College London reported in the journal, *NeuroImage*, that romantic love suppresses "neural activity associated with critical social assessment of other people and negative emotions." It seems that once we get close to another person—once we fall in love with them—our brain has a reduced need to assess their character and to harbor negative emotions towards them. Our love is blind. It is love we feel. It is not love we see.

It is our profound belief that the notion of "love is blind" has much merit. It is nature's way of allowing us to express our love for another person because we feel that love for them in our heart and in our soul. Our feelings of love are unconditional at the point we express them. Romantic love is blind, but that is not a bad thing.

Here is our twist on this intriguing notion. When you kiss someone you love in a romantic way, do you keep your eyes open or shut? Our bet—you close your eyes. Isn't this the essence of "love is blind?" You do not have to see the one you love to know you love them. You accept it on blind faith. And you kiss them without fear, without any sense of danger. You love them, if you will, blindly.

For almost four decades, we have interviewed thousands of couples that were in love. We have found many, many common characteristics that were pervasive throughout these loving relationships. Most notably, however, those in love, those truly in love, had love that transcended anything you could see or touch with your hand. Their love was love based on trust. Their love was unconditional love. Their love was love based on feelings that were heart-felt. Their love was so strong and so deep, it had become blind love.

It is okay to express your love openly, freely, unequivocally, honestly, and yes, blindly. What you feel in your heart does not need eyes to see.

The romantic 1955 movie, *Love is a Many Splendored Thing*, is the story of an American reporter who falls in love with a Eurasian doctor. And as you might have guessed, they encounter prejudice from both of their families. Such prejudice was, unfortunately, all too common in 1955. It is all too common in 2018.

People in love, it seems, do not always find a blind or colorblind world. That's too bad. Love is love. People who are in love, love each other irrespective of their race, creed, color, or national origin. True love between two people is colorblind—never forget that! Love does not see color, it only sees love.

In our research and travels we have often encountered people in love who have suffered the "slings and arrows of misfortune" because their relationship was a bi-racial one, or in many cases, a multi-racial relationship. Often times, there are people who observe others in love, but they do not always just see love. They see race. They see people who are different. Their prejudices take over. The dark side of some takes over. Too bad.

During the film, Love is a Many Splendored Thing, some intensely romantic meetings occur on a high and windswept hill. The song lyrics are clearly audible during many parts of the film.

This intensely romantic song touches the heart. It touched our heart. It will touch yours. It goes like this:

> *Once on a high and windy hill,*
> *In the morning mist, two lovers kissed,*
> *And the world stood still.*

You see, two people in love know their love for each other is timeless. They know their love is unconditional. They know it transcends everything else, even prejudice. Love between two people who are truly in love trumps everything else.

There is another line from the song that we think is particularly lovely:

> *Love is nature's way of giving.*
> *A reason to be living.*

Love must be shared. Love must be enjoyed. Love, quite frankly, is nature's way of telling people in love that they have many reasons to live – that they have many reasons to spend their life with the one they love.

There is another message about love. Love, when it comes your way, must be embraced. When you fall in love, you must seize the moment. Love does not always wait. When you fall in love, when you feel it completely, you must seize the moment:

> *Love is a many splendored thing*
> *It's the April rose that only grows in the early spring.*

When you fall in love, when you fall deeply in love, there is a good chance it will be forever. True love is between two individuals who see only love when they gaze into each other's eyes. Those in love do not see race, color, national origin, or prejudice. They see only love.

Love is a many splendored thing. Love is truly blind to those in love, and it should be to anyone who observes those in love.

Nicknames:
The Private Code for Love

*Nicknames are a private code
for saying, "I Love You."*

OVER OUR **52** YEARS OF
marriage we have met thousands of couples that deeply loved each
other. Nearly every one of them had an affectionate nickname for
each other—a sort of private "code" for saying, "I love you."

Some of the nicknames are ones you have probably heard many
times before—"lovey-dovey," "sweetie-pie," "sugar," "snookie-poo,"
"honey," "darling," "sweetness," "sweetpea," "baby girl," "lover boy,"
"sunshine," "sugarplum," "baby-doll," "hey, handsome," "hey, beautiful," and so forth.

Some of the nicknames are unusual and funny. Names like
"Butch" in reference to a very petite wife seem unusual, but to her
husband, it is an endearing term. "Snookems," in reference to a very
manly-man does not compute with most people, but to his wife, the
term is an expression of love and affection. And the list goes on.

Over the years, the funniest "affectionate" nickname we ever
heard was from the wife who lovingly referred to her husband as,
"turkey-fart." It is not important to understand the origin of
"turkey-fart." What is important is that the name has special

meaning to the husband and wife team that coined it. You see, love has a private code. People in love understand! Nicknames are a private code for saying, "I Love You."

Seasons of Baseball and Love

Over the years we have marveled at the parallels between the seasons of the year, and baseball and love.

SPRING HAS SPRING! IN THE Spring, all things are possible, every team can win the Pennant, and love is born! In so many ways, Spring is a metaphor for love, and hope, and the boundless promise of the dawn of a new season. In so many ways, the game of baseball speaks to all of these. And lest you think we are base-ball fans—we are!

First, do you remember that old familiar song, "Take me out to the ball game?" According to some reputable sources it is the third most sung song in America. One and two are "Happy Birthday" and "The Star Spangled Banner," respec-tively. We can find no evidence to dispute this notion.

And while most people are familiar with the chorus, almost no one has heard the rest of the popular song written by Jack Norworth in 1908 and revised in 1927. We have quoted the rest of the song below from the 1927 version.

Nelly Kelly loved baseball games,
Knew the players, knew all their names.

You could see her there ev'ry day,
Shout "Hurray" when they'd play.
Her boyfriend by the name of Joe
Said, "To Coney Isle, dear, let's go,"
Then Nelly started to fret and pout,
And to him, I heard her shout:

Chorus
"Take me out to the ball game,
Take me out on to the crowds;
Buy me some peanuts and Cracker Jacks,
I don't care if I never get back.
Let me root, root, root for the home team,
If they don't win, it's a shame.
For it's one, two, three strikes, you're out,
At the old ball game."

Nelly Kelly was in love with Joe. But being the independent minded women she apparently was, she told Joe she would rather go to a baseball game with him than join him for a day at Coney Island in New York City.

For those of you who may not know, Coney Island is a neighborhood in the Big Apple and it is home to one of the most well-known and longest running amusement parks in the United States. During the summer, in particular, lovers flock to Coney Island for roller coaster rides, cotton candy, hot dogs, and romance. It is a destination for lovers both young and old. You can lose all of your cares and woes at Coney Island, if only for a day. A lot of budding romances have taken seed at Coney Island, that's for sure. But Nelly Kelly it seems found love in the Spring at the baseball park. More on this notion a little later.

As a metaphor for love, the seasons of the year speak to love in all the right ways. The seed of love is planted in the

Spring, begins to grow as it is nourished by April showers. It blossoms into a beautiful flower in May. It is nurtured through the Spring and Summer, matures in the Fall, and settles in for Winter. Love has its seasons. Love has its Spring of birth, its Summer of love, its Fall of maturity, and its Winter of warmth by a crackling fireplace. Love is a many splendored thing. Love is a many seasoned thing.

Now we come to baseball. Ever notice how baseball fans become convinced in the Spring that this is the year their team is going to win the World Series. Optimism abounds. On Opening Day all things seem possible. The grass is dark green and freshly manicured, the stadium is squeaky clean, the smell of great food permeates the air, and the crack of the bat is a sound you have missed for far too long. When baseball season begins in the Spring, life begins again for young and old alike. Baseball begins in Spring for a reason! And so does love.

Over the years we have marveled at the parallels between the seasons of the year, and baseball and love. Nelly Kelly certainly had it right, "Take me out to the ballgame." She had it all—someone to love, her favorite game, and the seasons of love, life, and baseball to enjoy. May you enjoy your seasons of baseball and love as we have.

What Does Love Look Like?

You can't fake love.
True love can be seen, felt,
observed, and heard.

WHILE WE HAVE WRITTEN about how you will know you are in love, about how you will feel when you are in love, about the importance of the human touch in expressing love, and about how love sounds, we haven't yet shared our observations and findings about what love *looks like* until today! So here goes.

When we interview successfully married couples we spend a lot of time observing them while we listen carefully to what they say. We record our observations. We make note of what we see. Oh, what they say is important, but what we see is even more so.

We have discovered that you can learn much about love from observing two people in love. So what does love look like? What do two people in love "say" through their interactions with the one they love? When you observe couples in love, how do they act? How do they interact? What do their actions tell you about their love for each other? Well, here's something to think about.

People in love can be observed:

Listening to each other intently; holding hands while they walk or sit; touching each other often; teasing each other in playful ways; smiling at each other; hugging each other; sharing a meal from the same plate; opening doors for each other; putting their arms around each other; talking to each other with full eye contact; sitting together touching each other; sharing the care of their children; picking up each other's plates and meal residue after eating at fast food restaurants; and walking next to each other.

The way people in love gaze at each other—the way they look lovingly at each other—tells you there is a "look of love."

These are just a few of the telltale signs of people in love. We bet you can name more, but the important point to remember is that it is hard to fake love. People, who observe people in love or those just pretending to be in love, know the difference! There is without a doubt "a look of love."

So, friends, our message about love being "an accumulation of the little things" should come through loud and clear again. You can't fake love. True love can be seen, felt, observed, and heard. Keep these simple things in mind next time you think about love.

We close with the words of Burt Bacharach in his very popular song, "The Look of Love."

> *I can hardly wait to hold you*
> *Feel my arms around you*
> *How long I have waited*
> *Waited just to love you*
> *Now that I have found you*
> *Don't ever go.*

There is no doubt—you can SEE love. You can't hide it. You can't fake it. You can't fool those who observe your relationship with each other.

To love is to show your love by your actions. To say you are in love doesn't count for much unless you show your love. To look like love is, more often than not, to be in love.

WHAT ARE THE BENEFITS OF MARRIAGE?

IN MARRIAGE SIMPLE THINGS MATTER

The Benefits of Marriage

*You have many powerful reasons
to work hard to have
a long and happy marriage.*

*N*OW YOU KNOW THAT THE recipe for a successful marriage takes a lot of hard work doing the simple things each day, this chapter should convince you that it is absolutely worth whatever it takes for you to achieve a long-term successful marriage. After a lengthy review of the current research on the benefits of marriage, we have selected what we think are the top 10 reasons why you should work hard to achieve a happy successful marriage. It has been proven time and time again that your life can be improved in a great number of ways by staying in a successful long-term marriage!

Top 10 Benefits of Marriage:

Reason #1: You will live longer. The preponderance of evidence from research shows a relationship between longer life and being married. In fact, one study found that married men live an average of ten years longer and married women live an average of four years longer than those who are unmarried.

Reason #2: You will be healthier. There have been a great number of research studies throughout the world since 1987 demonstrating a positive relationship between being married and better physical health. The links between marriage and good physical health are overwhelming. Married individuals have lower rates of serious illness and are less likely to die in hospitals.

Reason #3: You will be happier. Married people report being happier than unmarried people. They are hopeful, happy and feel good about themselves. A multitude of studies demonstrate the same results. In fact, in a 10-year survey involving 14,000 adults, James Davis found that 40% of married individuals were happy with their life compared to only 15-20% of any of the unmarried groups.

Reason #4: You will experience higher levels of psychological health. Married people have lower rates of depression and schizophrenia than unmarried people. They are better balanced and less likely to experience mental illness.

Reason #5: You will have a built-in support system. Research indicates that individuals in a marriage feel supported, saying that they have someone to share their feelings and thoughts with. They always have someone they trust to confide in and to lean on in times of need.

Reason #6: You will be less likely to abuse drugs or alcohol. Numerous studies indicate that married individuals are less likely than unmarried persons to engage in risky behaviors including the use of drugs or alcohol because of their feelings of responsibility.

Reason #7: Your earnings will be greater. Numerous studies found that married men's earnings are significantly greater than unmarried men's earning. The most recent studies of women's earning power demonstrate that married women earn more than unmarried women even when their husband's income is not considered part of their earnings. The vast majority of the studies take all of the various possible factors into consideration and the results still demonstrate greater earnings for married individuals than for unmarried ones.

Reason #8: You will save more money. With enduring marriages couples tend to be more financially responsible. In the United States married individuals in their 50s and 60s have a net worth per person roughly twice that of other unmarried individuals.

Reason #9: You will have sex more often and enjoy it more. Physically and emotionally married couples report a greater satisfaction with sex then their unmarried counterparts. Married couples also have sexual intimacy more often than unmarried couples.

Reason #10: Your children will be healthier, do better academically and have less emotional problems. Children living in families with married parents are more likely to have proper health care, better nutrition and less stress to deal with at home. These children have less serious illnesses and grew up healthier than children not raised in households with married parents.

On average, children who are raised in households with stable marriages enjoy better developmental outcomes than children raised in households with unmarried individuals. These children have significantly better grades, test scores and overall success in school than their counterparts raised in households with unmarried individuals.

The research indicates that children living with married parents have less reported behavioral problems at school or at home than children who do not. They experience better psychological health than children raised in households with unmarried parents or guardians. Your children are less likely to engage in risky behaviors if you remain in a stable marriage. For example, sexual activity, drug, alcohol and weapons use are less likely to occur with children raised in married households. Children have a better opportunity to grow to fully functional adults if married parents raise them.

Linda Gallagher and Maggie Waite, after analyzing the results of their comprehensive study on the benefits of marriage in 1990, suggested that there should be a similar warning about not being married as the Surgeon General's warning on cigarette packages. They want divorce decrees to carry the warning label, "Not being married can be hazardous to your health." They could not have said it better.

A 2014 study by the world-renowned Gallup Organization confirms the results of our research, as well as multiple other studies conducted over the decades regarding marriage benefits. Gallup's telephone interviews of over 131,000 randomly selected adults ages 18 and older living in all 50 USA states and the District of Columbia, highlights the conclusion that "Married Americans tend to have higher well-being than non-married Americans, particularly those who are divorced or separated . . ."

The bottom line, Gallup found that the increased drug/meditation use that is designed to help a man or a women (particularly a women) relax and reduce their stress, is linked to divorce and separation. Incidences of drug/medication/alcohol abuse appears in some three in 10 for separated or divorced Americans—some 13% higher than "adults who are married or, in domestic partnerships, or single . . ."

In reviewing the Gallup study, we think the best summary paragraph from their report is this, "Marriage is a associated with higher well-being for both men and women, particularly when compared with divorce or separation. Entering a marriage can foster a sense of purpose through a shared perspective on life and a need to support another person. Similarly, marriage can expand a person's social connections and relationships, increase household wealth, and lead to a more permanent housing selection and a related connection to the community. In addition, multiple studies have confirmed that married adults have better health outcomes, likely attributable to reduced stress and having a partner to encourage healthy behaviors and to hold one accountable for choices affecting one's health." We couldn't have said it better ourselves!

Trust us when we say that Gallup's research and interview protocols are without equal. Gallup trained us in the marriage interview techniques we have employed for over 30 years. We learned from the best!

When you consider what social science research tells us about the benefits of being married and what our research reveals about the importance of the seven characteristics of successful marriages, you have many powerful reasons to work hard to have a long and happy marriage.

Living the American Dream

*Being married is still a major part
of the American dream.*

W<small>E ARE OFTEN ASKED</small>
the question, is being happily married for a lifetime still part of the American dream? The answer is, YES.

In fact, there is more than an 80% chance that everyone in America who is living today will be married at least once in their lifetime. Marriage is a major part of how people define themselves in America today. One of the first questions on almost any form is, "Are you married or single?"

When talking about their future, young adults still aspire to find the love of their lives, get married and live happily ever after. All you have to do is watch television, read the Internet blogs, go to the movies, or look at the many Bride's magazines, to understand that young people today still believe that marriage is an important part of defining who they are as a human being.

Marriage is still one of the greatest contributors to social order in America today. And the fact of the matter is this—marriage is the most profound commitment to lasting love that exists. Those who question its importance ignore the facts.

The fact is that the national per capita divorce rate has declined steadily since its peak in 1981 and is now at its lowest level since

1979. The fact that the per capita divorce has declined should be cause for celebration.

Over the years we have seen a positive trend developing and it is highly encouraging to us. The good news—more and more couples are committed to making their marriage work! In a society that is often characterized as "a disposable society," marriage has too many benefits to be routinely disposed of.

The chances of making marriage work can be greatly improved by understanding what factors have major implications for the risk of divorce. **Barbara Whitehead and David Popenoe in their book entitled The State of Our Unions (2004) reported the following:**

1. Couples with annual incomes over $50,000 (vs. under $25,000) have a reduced risk of divorce of 30%. The message here is that couples contemplating marriage would be well advised to have income-producing jobs with stability before they get married.

2. Couples who have a baby seven months or more after marriage (vs. before marriage) have a reduced risk of divorce of 24%. The message here should be clear—bring children into the world when your marriage is ready.

3. Couples who are 25 years of age (vs. under 18) have a 24% less risk of divorce. The American divorce rate has been going down since 1981 because people in love are waiting longer to get married. Gaining education, experience, and the wisdom that comes with age will certainly contribute to the success of a marriage.

4. Couples that consider themselves religious or spiritual (vs. not) are 14% less likely to get divorced. Faith and spirituality contribute to the sense of oneness felt by successfully married couples.

5. Couples who have some college (vs. high-school dropout) have a 13% less chance of divorce. Education almost always leads to enlightenment and understanding, and more tolerance for the views of others, so critically important in successful marriages.

In summary, reasonably well-educated couples with a decent income, who are religious or spiritual, who wait awhile to have children, who come from intact families, and who marry later in life (25 and beyond), have a greatly reduced chance of divorce.

Considering that most adult Americans will be married at least once in their lifetime, it is nice to know that there is much we can do as individuals and as couples in love to improve the chances of making marriage work—to make marriage successful.

Marriage Is a Status Symbol

Marriage has become an important indicator of a successful personal life in the United States and around the world

WHY HAS MARRIAGE become an important indicator of a successful personal life?.

Let's face it, from all of the available research we have reviewed about marriage and its benefits, the one benefit that stands out most is this—more and more people who get married are getting married "because marriage is a status symbol." As long-time marriage advocates and researchers, we are most pleased by this recently identified benefit of marriage.

Over the years, we have identified many benefits of marriage. The fact of the matter is this—marriage has become an important indicator of a successful personal life in the United States and around the world! Marriage is the single greatest contributor to social order on planet Earth and the most profound commitment to lasting love that exists. Those who question its importance ignore the facts.

Statistically, there is substantial support for our point of view. According to the best estimates we can find, there were over 45,000,000 marriages worldwide last year. There were approximately 9,000,000 divorces in the same year. If you do the math you can see that worldwide, marriages outnumber divorces by a ratio of

5 to 1. Stated clearly and succinctly, there were five marriages for every one divorce in the world last year. Hardly sounds like the death of marriage to us!

As love and marriage experts, we have seen a positive trend developing over the years and it is highly encouraging. The good news is more and more couples are committed to making their marriage work! In a society that is often characterized as "a disposable society," marriage has too many benefits to be routinely "disposed."

Interestingly, it is clear that some 75% (three-quarters) of folks who get married today met the traditional ways (work and school, friends and family, church/synagogue/place of worship). Just 20% get married who meet through bars and social events, and from an on-line dating sites. Traditional ways of meeting a future spouse continue to dominate for those who ultimately get married.

Marriage Has Huge Economic Advantages

Among the principle advantages of marriage is shared financial stability—now and in the future.

*W*E HAVE FOUND IN OUR almost four decades of research on successful marriage around the world that being married has huge economic advantages. Doubters have challenged us to "prove it!" The latest proof is a recently release special report by the Heritage Foundation entitled, Marriage: America's Greatest Weapon Against Child Poverty.

Being married has tons of advantages—love, companionship, children, shared responsibility, financial stability, and the like. But in the end, financial stability in the modern era may, in fact, drive almost everything else. We know this—among the principle advantages of marriage, is shared financial stability—now and in the future.

Here are the facts. The number one economic advantage of marriage is income! According to recent data reported by the U.S. Census Bureau and by the Heritage Foundation, the poverty rate for single parents with children in the USA was "37.1 percent." The poverty "rate for married couples with children was "6.8 percent."

The Heritage Report goes on to say that being "raised in a married family reduces a child's probability of living in poverty by nearly 82%." Need we say more about being married and its positive impact on our children?

The sad reality is this—in 1964, more than 9 out of 10 children born in the USA were born to married parents. By 2010 that number had dropped to 6 in 10—a one-third drop. If you wanted to know the single greatest cause of childhood poverty, look no further.

The terrible truth of the matter is this—the number of children born out of wedlock had increased to just over 40% by 2010. And make no mistake about it, most of the births of our "out of wedlock" children have come to women who have a high school degree or less—those women who have the most difficult time going it alone in the world—those who are most likely to raise their children in poverty.

Here's the bottom line: the huge increases in child poverty are twofold—out of wedlock childbearing and increases in single parenthood. According to data from the U.S. Census Bureau, some 71% of poor families with children are not married. So we ask this simple question—why would we continue to have children out of wedlock? What favors are we doing for our children? Why do we want to have children born in poverty? Why would we not want our children to be born out of poverty and with a reasonable chance of success?

Here is one undeniable fact—children born of married women who have some level of education beyond high school are much more likely to be born out of poverty. When it comes to child welfare, when it comes to combating poverty, get married!!

Now, on to another important fact in the battle for marriage—income, income, income!

According to recent statistics, more than HALF of single mother families have an annual income of less than $25,000 per year. The median income for single mother families is also about $25,000. But imagine this—the median family income for married couple families is nearly $78,000—more than THREE TIMES the income of single mother families!

Unbelievably, 41% of single-mother families live in poverty compared to only 9% for married-couple families—FOUR times as many! Moreover, 40% of single mothers are poor and nearly two-thirds of single mothers receive Food Stamps.

In the final analysis, married couples in the USA are no longer a majority according to the U.S. Census Bureau. In our estimation, that is a sad situation. This drop in marriage explains more than any other phenomenon, the substantial increases in child poverty and in the significant income disparity of married versus unmarried individuals.

In the end, the choice is yours. Do you want your children to live in poverty? Do you want to live in poverty yourself? Do you like the income difference between being married or not?

Here's the deal—we do not advocate marriage for the sake of marriage, for eliminating poverty, or to address income disparity. We DO advocate marriage for the stability it provides our children, for the income stability it provides our families, and for the many positive opportunities marriage provides, in general, for all of us.

Healthy Habits, Healthy Love

Seven areas of focus can help you begin developing healthy living habits.

*T*HE HEALTH BENEFITS OF marriage, both physical and emotional, have been well documented since the 1850's when a British epidemiologist by the name of William Farr concluded that the unmarried die "in undue proportion" to those who are married. He offered, "The single individual is more likely to be wrecked on his voyage than the lives joined together in matrimony." We would offer that his conclusions of a century and a half ago still apply today.

Dr. Edward P. Ehlinger, commissioner of the Minnesota Department of Health, concluded the following in an article on September 22, 2012: "Recent studies confirm Farr's observation of lower mortality rates and better physical and mental health among married individuals. Married men and women have lower rates of depression, Alzheimer's disease, cardiovascular disease, smoking, substance abuse and cancer. After controlling for other factors, married couples have higher levels of cognitive functioning, happiness and life satisfaction. All the health benefits of marriage are consistent across age, race and education groups."

His conclusion is powerful and totally consistent with our research on marriage for nearly four decades. Married couples are healthier, happier, more mentally well adjusted, more socially adjusted, and better off economically, as are their children.

There should be nothing surprising or Earth-shattering about these notions. It stands to reason that those who have somebody ("Everybody needs somebody, sometime.") will be happier, healthier, and more socially well-adjusted.

Human beings are social animals—they want and need someone to spend their life with. When they have someone, they are, in fact, healthier—on virtually all fronts. Why would anyone argue against something so obvious? Why would anyone deny such a well-known truth? It is clear that the best marriages understand the health benefits of marriage. To deny these benefits is to bury your head in the sand.

So why does being married translate into important health benefits? Simple really—people who are married help take care of each other's health and here is how they do it.

Couples have the recognition that the health of you and your spouse is critical to your relationship, both short-term and long-term. Successfully married couples watch out for each other's eating habits, exercise, vitamins, and medicines because they know that their relationship with each other is enhanced when they are healthy. If you get married young, there is a tendency to ignore the health risk factors because you think you will live forever. Instead, begin thinking long-term and focus on developing healthy habits both physically and mentally.

Seven areas of focus can help you begin developing healthy living habits:

1. Learn to cook healthy meals together. Enjoy each other's company while you spend extra time communicating with each other. Find recipes that are fun to fix and fun to eat together. A good way to start is to try a few of the salad recipes we have included in our book, "Building a Love that Lasts" (Jossey-Bass/Wiley). They are from happily married couples all over the world who realized that healthy eating benefitted their relationship with each other

2. ***Develop a regular exercise program together.*** It doesn't matter if it is just walking together in the evening after work or riding bicycles in the park or going to the gym or swimming. What matters is that you do it together and commit to staying on a regular program to enhance your physical and mental health. Yes, exercise does make a positive impact on your mental health.

3. ***Focus on maintaining good psychological health for yourself and your spouse.*** Having a shoulder to cry on or someone to lean on when things get tough can keep you from the depths of depression. Life can throw unbelievable challenges in your path, so having your spouse as your best friend can provide both of you with the support you need to make it through the tough times together. Like the song goes, "that's what friends are for."

4. ***For a long life together, take a balanced regimen of vitamins.*** Don't fool yourself into believing that you will get all of your nutrition by eating a well balanced diet. While it might help, with the stress in today's life it is critical that you make sure that you get the required vitamins and minerals with good vitamin supplements.

5. ***Eliminate bad habits.*** In other words, cut back on your foods containing refined sugars, white flour, salt, food additives such as food coloring, artificial flavorings and preservatives. Stop smoking. Limit your intact of alcohol to 1-2 drinks per day. Get off the couch. Get more consistent sleep.

6. ***Get regular annual medical check-ups.*** Encourage your spouse to get a regular physical check-up annually by sched-

uling your appointments on the same day. Preventative care is far superior to having to deal with a health issue that went undetected for a long period of time.

7. ***Make living a healthy well-balanced life a priority.*** Just like everything else in life, you have to set your goals and priorities focused on what is important to you. While you may not have any health issues yet, if you develop healthy living habits that focus on maintaining a healthy well-balanced life style, you have a far greater chance of celebrating your golden years together.

You see, the health benefits of marriage come about as a result of the relationship between two people in love. It does take two to Tango. Marriage has many health benefits because of the behaviors of those who entered into the sacred bond of marriage. Honestly, does this surprise you?

There are many health benefits of marriage. Take advantage of them. You won't regret it.

Love well. Love healthy.

Imagine Life Without
Someone to Share It With

Don't grow old by yourself.
Find someone to love.
Life is too short to spend it alone.

*T*HE BEST MARRIAGE ADVICE we can offer after all these years of research and writing is this, DON'T GROW OLD BY YOURSELF! Life is too short to spend it alone.

The simple truth is this—growing old alone is a death sentence. Such a state is worse than having a dreaded disease. Trust us when we say this, being alone at the end of days is a fate worse than death. Here's why.

Okay, we are madly in love after all these years! We have been married for 52 years and we cannot imagine life without each other. We are each other's constant companions and wouldn't want it any other way!

But we must admit, we often think about "all the lonely people" who are, in their advanced age, all alone. They have no one with whom to share his or her days and nights with. Worse yet, no one to share their advancing age with.

On a recent trip to our neighborhood Starbuck's we were struck by the number of people who were there by themselves. These weren't old people with a dead spouse, they were people in their 20's, 30's, and 40's who were **accompanied by no one**! They sat by themselves sipping their latte, reading the newspaper or a book, or checking their social media accounts on their iPhone.

In all the times we have gone to this bustling coffee shop we noticed the same thing, but never did anything about it until today. We decided to follow up our experience by sharing our thoughts about seeing so many lonely and alone people in one space.

Is this the new America? Is this the way it's going to be in the 21st Century? The answers to these questions are worth pursuing we think.

We begin by asking this simple question—why are there so many people spending their days alone? Is it our imagination or are we truly on to some profound changes going on in our society?

It is clear; the rate of those getting married in our society is declining. According to the University of Virginia study entitled *The State of Our Unions 2010*, marriage has been on the decline since the 1960's.

For example, marriage today among white males and white females has dropped some 20% overall since the 60's.

The marriage decline is even more pronounced for Black males during this same time frame where marriage is down 40% overall.

Even more dramatic is the marriage decline for Black women where marriage is down over 50% since the 1960's.

Part of the aforementioned declines is due to people getting married at an older age than in the 1960's. People getting married at the ages of 15, 16, 17, and 18 are much less prevalent in our society today than they were in 1960, and that fact is probably a good thing.

The significant declines in marriage among African-Americans and among the American middle class are the two most troubling declines. While getting married later in life is a good thing that has led to higher success rates in marriage, not getting married at all is not good for people and not good for America. In Middle America and among the African-American community, marriage is in trouble!

These are the five major conclusions one can draw from the University of Virginia study:

1. Marriage is an emerging dividing line between America's moderately educated middle and those with college degrees.

2. Marital quality is declining for the moderately educated middle but not for their highly educated peers.

3. Divorce rates are up for moderately educated Americans, relative to those who are highly educated.

4. The moderately educated middle is dramatically more likely than highly educated Americans to have children outside of marriage.

5. The children of highly educated parents are now more likely than in the recent past to be living with their mother and father, while children with moderately educated parents are far less likely to be living with their mother and father.

Their most stunning summary statement of the report reads as follows:

"So the United States is increasingly a separate and unequal nation when it comes to the institution of marriage. Marriage is in danger of becoming a luxury good attainable only to those with the material and cultural means to grab hold of it. The marginalization of marriage in

Middle America is especially worrisome, because this institution has long served the American experiment in democracy as an engine of the American Dream, a seedbed of virtue for children, and one of the few sources of social solidarity in a nation that otherwise prizes individual liberty."

Just imagine—the most fundamental and central component of American society—the glue of our socialization process for the total of American history (and for nearly 6000 years of recorded world history) has been marriage. There has been no more important "glue" for the social structure of America than marriage. Any threat to the sanctity or importance of marriage between two people puts our society at risk.

In the end, we believe the University of Virginia should have added a 6th conclusion: *There is great danger for the Republic when people in love choose to stay "single" and not make the commitment of love so prevalent in our history as a nation.*

Don't be fooled into thinking that the great social traditions of America will continue without marriage. Don't think that spending most of your life without someone is good for you or good for America. Everybody needs somebody. Of that you can be sure.

Marriage between two people who love each other has been an enduring element in the success of America from the beginning of our great country. There are many reasons to support marriage as an institution, but perhaps the most important reason is this—you will not grow old by yourself—the most compelling reason of all in our estimation.

In the end, it is of utmost importance to all of us to have someone who loves us, has our best interests at heart, commits to being our life's companion, is our advocate, stays with us through thick and thin, and is there for us during the ending stages of our life.

We are reminded again of the lyrics from Neil Diamond's 1972 song, *Morningside,* "The old man died. And no one cried. They simply turned away" (Prophet Music, Inc. (ASCAP)).

No one wants to grow old alone. We would dare say that most everyone wants someone to be their companion when they grow old. To cry for them when they die.

Don't grow old by yourself. Find someone to love. Life is too short to spend it alone.

WHAT ARE THE SIMPLE THINGS THAT MATTER?

IN MARRIAGE SIMPLE THINGS MATTER

The Simple Things that Matter

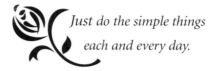

*Just do the simple things
each and every day.*

*I*T IS AN ESTABLISHED FACT— successful love is based on an accumulation of the "simple things." We can state unequivocally, if you want your marriage or your relationship to succeed, you have to do the simple things each and every day.

To get you started right away, we put together a list of 50 examples of simple things that matter in love and marriage. This list is your first step in making your love survive and thrive over a lifetime together.

1. Take long walks together.
2. Snuggle in the morning before you get out of bed.
3. Recognize kindness with a thank you.
4. Call when you are going to be late.
5. Be generous with your time for each other.
6. Watch a sunset together.
7. Compliment your lover about something he/she did today that made him/her special.
8. Hold hands often.
9. Bring home flowers for him/her when it is not a special occasion.

10. Leave a sticky note on your lover's wallet or purse telling him/her to come home safely to you because you love him/her.

11. Ask your spouse about their dreams and desires for your future together.

12. Open doors for each other.

13. Bike ride together, bringing a picnic lunch for a secluded spot along the way.

14. Walk your dog together while discussing the issues of the day.

15. Fix your lover breakfast in bed for no special reason.

16. Say "I love you" several times during each day.

17. Treat your lover with courtesy at all times.

18. Help clean off the table and do the dishes after dinner.

19. Compliment your lover's cooking.

20. Tell him or her each day why he or she means so much to you.

21. Take your spouse to their favorite restaurant in the middle of the week.

22. Touch your mate 100 times a day.

23. Surprise your spouse by bringing lunch when least expected.

24. Prepare meals together as often as you can.

25. Spend an evening listening to music and making a playlist of your favorite songs together.

26. Upend expectancies and delight your lover. Make things exciting and fun.

27. Always point out the positive attributes of your lover, both at home and in public.

28. Give your husband or wife a massage or a back rub.

29. Look directly into your lover's eye when you are having a conversation.

30. Be your lover's best cheerleader for their accomplishments.

31. Plan a bubble bath together and see where it leads.

32. Turn off your iPhone during meals together.

33. Talk about everything. No topic is too small or too big. There are no sacred cows.

34. Always demonstrate respect for each other in your words and in your actions.

35. Schedule your annual physicals on the same day.

36. Plan a week of healthy meals together with foods that you both enjoy.

37. Write your husband/wife a love letter and leave it for him/her to find in their underwear drawer.

38. Sit down and go over the finances together before you pay the bills for the month.

39. Take your lover to a movie, putting your arm around them like you used do when you were dating.

40. Go for a boat ride, car ride or train ride that isn't planned and doesn't have an itinerary.

41. Write personal Valentine's Day cards.

42. Turn off the television and talk to each other.

43. Sing a song together and to each other.

44. Go to Disneyland—just the two of you.

45. Plant flowers together.

46. Share a tuna melt.

47. Kiss each other passionately.

48. Go to the zoo together.

49. Share a shower

50. Sit in your porch swing and gaze at the stars.

You see, the simple things do matter. Change your relationship and your life in positive ways by doing the simple things. Start today.

While these 50 ideas are good examples of the simple things that can get you started, the remaining chapters of this book are filled with powerful ideas about simple things that can sustain your love for a lifetime.

Love IS Having to Say You're Sorry

This simple notion may very well be one of the great truths about loving, successful, and long-lasting relationships.

THE MOST FAMOUS LINE FROM the wildly popular 1970 book (and subsequent movie), *Love Story,* by Erich Segal is, "Love means never having to say you are sorry." As a *New York Times* number one bestseller, the book became the top selling work of fiction for all of 1970 in the United States, and was translated into more than 20 languages worldwide according to Wikipedia. The motion picture of the same name was the number one box office attraction of 1971."

The opening narrative of the book by the main character, Oliver, says, "What can you say about a twenty-five-year-old girl who died? That she was beautiful and brilliant? That she loved Mozart and Bach, the Beatles, and me?" The rest of the book is just as riveting, trust us on that.

Love Story is a beautiful story. If you have any heart at all, you will cry your eyes out after reading the book or watching the movie. In the end, Jenny dies and we are all heart-broken. Lessons abound.

Segal's work is a true romantic story about love, life, and death. It touched the hearts of everyone who read the book or saw the movie. The problem is, the basic premise of the most famous line of the book is "Love is never having to say you are sorry, is wrong. Love IS having to say you are sorry!

Love Story is a book about one of the great love stories of the 20th Century. There are many lessons about love and life. But the most famous lesson of the book is a lesson you should not learn, and we wonder from time to time if many of the failed marriages over the past half century in the United States and around the world might in some way be related to the notion that being in love does not require you to apologize when you do or say something wrong.

What is so confusing about the message of the book and the movie is this—because we are in love with someone, does that make us immune from apologizing for our bad behavior? Just because we are married or engaged to someone, are we exempt from saying **I'm sorry** when we hurt our lover's feelings or disappoint them with our words and actions.

From time to time in any loving relationship, things can go awry. People who love each other get angry. They yell at each other and say hurtful things. We all make mistakes in judgment. Sometimes we show our dark side to the people we love. And frankly, there are times when we make fools out of ourselves around the ones we love.

When two people love each other, they feel more comfortable discussing perplexing or challenging problems. They are willing to address the tough issues head on. Why, because they trust each other more than they trust any other human being. They feel comfortable with the one they love. And because their comfort level is so high they often say and do things to each other that are hurtful. But because they love each other and trust each other, does it give them carte-blanche license to say and do whatever they want, even if it is damaging or hurtful? Of course not! But the reality is that it happens and the wounds can be deep. Feelings can be hurt. Relationships strained.

Which leads us to the most important point of this chapter—love IS having to say you are sorry. There are no ifs, ands, or buts about it. When you engage in behavior, actions, or words that are hurtful and damaging in your relationship with the one you love, you not only should apologize, you MUST do so! In our humble opinion, no two people who profess to love each other can ever take the position that they don't have to apologize to each other for saying and doing hurtful things. And, never take the position that "Oh, they know I love them. I don't have to say I'm sorry." The latter is one of the most egregious of all sins you can commit in your relationship with the one you love—taking them for granted.

In the end, there is only one correct action to take when you hurt the one you love. You must say you are sorry. Contrary to what Jenny said to Oliver in *Love Story*, LOVE IS HAVING TO SAY YOU ARE SORRY. This simple notion may very well be one of the great truths about loving, successful, and long-lasting relationships—one of the great truths about marriages and relationships that celebrate their golden anniversaries.

Communication Is at the Heart of All Great Marriages

Successful couples report to us that they never felt invalidated by their spouse.

*H*APPILY MARRIED COUPLES attribute their marital success first and foremost to the fact that they have honed their communication skills over time. They report a high level of satisfaction with the way they communicate. They talk about everything and anything with each other—they have "No Sacred Cows" in their marriage.

So, what are the lessons we have learned over the past 37 years of research from our interviews throughout the world with couples that communicate effectively on just about every level? As we poured over our interview notes from thousands of couples, **five important actions emerged.**

> 1. *Effective marital communication always begins with proper engagement and in a proper context.* Talking about serious matters cannot occur effectively when dealing with chaos, such as a blaring television, crying baby, or talking on your iPhone.

2. There is proper etiquette to follow in effective communication. Lower your voices, speak in a calm manner, make eye contact, listen intently and seek clarification if you don't understand. Refrain from blaming, accusing, calling names, making nasty remarks or getting defensive.

3. Discussions about serious issues must always begin with agreement about what the issues really are. Work to identify the issue, establish the parameters of the discussion, and agree to solve the problem together.

4. A fruitful conversation about important matters always begins with the brainstorming of ideas. It is important to get your respective ideas out on the table. Talk about the relative strengths and weaknesses of each. Agree on ideas worth exploring.

5. Never, we repeat, never be judgmental when debating issues with your mate. Instantly passing judgment on an idea is usually the death of open and honest debate between two people.

The thousands of successfully married couples we have interviewed report to us that they never felt invalidated by their spouse, that they always felt their arguments were heard, and that their opinions always mattered. Learn the simple lessons of communication that these wonderful couples practice everyday of their lives together.

Toilet Seat Love

*Toilet Seat Love describes
just one of those simple things
that really matter.*

As WE SAY REPEATEDLY, the simple things matter in love and marriage. Do the simple things and your marriage or loving relationship will prosper.

Charley learned his lesson some 40 years ago! He grew up in a rural area of Missouri back when outhouses were more prevalent than toilets that flushed! When we first got married some 52 years ago, Charley, "the consummate gentleman" as Liz refers to him, had to learn an important lesson about toilet seats.

As it turns out, toilet seats are designed to protect women and save marriages! There are four kinds of husbands when it comes to *Toilet Seat Love.* Here they are, briefly described.

First, husband number one goes to the bathroom. He lifts the seat and goes, then replaces the seat in its down position. Wife loves husband when he does this! The marriage is saved!

Husband number two fails to lift the seat and, thusly, goes ON the seat. But, being a kind and respectful husband, he cleans up his mess with a handful of Kleenex. Wife still loves husband but not as much.

The third kind of husband goes to the bathroom, doesn't lift the seat, goes ON seat, doesn't clean seat, and wife sits in his mess later that day. Wife is not happy with husband! Trust us on this.

The fourth kind of husband raises the seat before he goes, but leaves seat in the upright position when he is done. Later that day, wife sits in the toilet bowl and the impact splashes toilet bowl contents on the floor. Occasionally, she gets stuck in bowl and needs assistance in getting out. Wife does not love husband when he does this. The marriage is in jeopardy!

We hope you enjoyed the levity of this little story but, more importantly, you find its meaning to be helpful as you think about the little things that make your loving relationship with someone else thrive. *Toilet Seat Love* describes just one of those simple things that really matter. Always remember that lasting relationships and successful marriages are built on an accumulation of the simple things.

The One Essential Element
of a Happy Marriage

*Trust is at the heart of
all successful marriages.*

RECENTLY, WE HAD a delightful radio interview with a Los Angeles station to promote our book, *How to Marry the Right Guy*. During the course of the interview the host ask us to share with him "the one thing" that is essential to all great marriages. There was no equivocation in our answer.

Trust is at the heart of all great marriages. When you fall in love, trust in the one you love becomes the very foundation of that relationship. Successfully married couples literally trust each other with their lives, their sacred honor, and their very being.

Now, here's the essence of this message—the best marriages we have discovered around the world over these past 37 years of research understand the importance that vulnerability plays in the ongoing development of trust within their heartfelt and loving relationship.

A marriage between two human beings is a complex entity. Make no mistake about that. And here's the truth—marriages do not start out great, they grow over time. How, you ask?

Vulnerability is the answer! People who trust each other completely are willing to be vulnerable with each other—they are willing "let their hair down" with each other. They are willing to be totally honest with each other. They are completely and utterly willing to share their true feelings with each other. The strength of great marriages begins with open, honest, and truthful communication.

And like nearly all of the most happily and successfully married couples we have interviewed around the world, they understand that sharing their true feelings, opinions, and assessments with each other, is the absolute and necessary prerequisite to building a love that lasts a lifetime.

So where does vulnerability come into the equation? When you allow yourself to be vulnerable with another human being you are expressing your trust in them to not betray you, make fun of you, ignore you, or minimize you.

To be vulnerable in a loving relationship is to be open, receptive, sensitive, and willing to shut down personal defenses in order to engage in honest communication. Only through non-defensive and open exchanges of information do people in love truly begin to grow their love and trust for each other. Let's face it, vulnerability is NOT a dirty word when it comes to love and marriage.

When you are willing to be vulnerable with someone you purport to love, you have reached the nirvana of your relationship. It is clear from our research that being willing to be vulnerable with the one you love is a necessary pre-condition for the creation of a strong and lasting loving relationship. And, trust is the prerequisite to being willing to be vulnerable in your relationship with the one you love.

Let us be bold—marriages do NOT grow and thrive without trust and without the willingness of the respective partners to allow themselves to be vulnerable with each other. Great marriages begin with trust and the willingness to be vulnerable.

Positive growth within great marriages begins with simple notions. Mutual trust and vulnerability are the essential components of great marriages. If these two components don't describe your relationship, reconsider it. The evidence from around the world is overwhelming and compelling.

Simple Things Matter
During the Holidays

*Every family has its own holiday traditions
and if your family is lucky they will carry
them on year after year after year.*

*T*RUTH IS, WE MISS OUR
parents and our grandparents. True to the natural course of life,
they are all gone now. They were parents in life and, in many ways,
parents in death. They all lived long lives. They all lived full and
productive lives. And they all loved the holiday season because of
the simple things.

The holiday season is truly a season for all. Nearly all faiths,
religions, and ways of life find something to celebrate during this
important season. Whatever your faith, whatever your beliefs,
always remember this—simple things matter during the holidays.

The most important part of the holiday season has to do with
the family traditions we have started along the way and that
continue from generation to generation. Many of those traditions
have to do with the food we prepare for those special holiday meals.
To this day, we make Grandma Uthe's time-honored German potato
salad every Christmas.

Years ago, Liz started a tradition all her own—making the best
turkey stuffing in the entire universe, and beyond! Our whole

family can't wait to scarf down generous portions of her delectable dressing. The turkey comes second!

Charley's grandma on his mother's side always put lemon drops wrapped in cellophane on the Christmas tree for the grandchildren. Aunt Vi placed cellophane wrapped chocolate drops on the tree as her annual tradition.

The family holiday tradition in Liz's family was stringing fresh popped popcorn. But the truth is they ate most of the popcorn before it got on the sting! Most popcorn stringing events ended with full tummies, a mess on the kitchen floor, and lots and lots and lots of laughter. Liz still tears up when she teaches the art of popcorn stinging to our two grandchildren.

When Charley was eight years old, his Dad put toy train tracks around the Christmas tree. It left indelible memories in his brain about his Dad and about the tradition he started.

And every Christmas when we decorate our Christmas tree with over 400 ornaments we have collected from around the world. we bake chocolate chip cookies!

Memories are made of this, that's for sure. Every family has its own holiday tradition and if your family is lucky they will carry them on year after year after year.

While we recognize that traditions vary from family to family, always remember this—carry them on. Have your own children learn them. Passing them from generation to generation reminds you every special holiday of those you have loved along the way, of those who were kind to you and expressed their love to you through their simple deeds. Traditions as a rule don't usually cost much money, but they last a lifetime.

Over the years, we have written much about the "simple things." And we have always reminded you that simple things matter in love and life. If you do the simple things day in an day out—simple acts of kindness, simple expressions of love, simple homemade gifts and cards, simple traditions—you will enrich not only your life but also the lives of others.

Too often in life, people who love each other make these mistakes:

- You send expensive flowers on an anniversary or holiday but fail to look the one you love in the eyes and tell him or her how much you love them.

- You shower the one you purport to love with expensive gifts instead giving them what they really want—your respect, your understanding, your embrace, your kiss and your time.

- You think that a store bought card is a good substitute for a homemade one!

- You give your children expensive toys when all they want is your love.

- You send grandma and grandpa a card when all they want is for you to call them on the phone.

And the list goes on.

Our final thought for today is this—No love has blossomed or been sustained without doing the simple things during the holidays.

iPhone Love

The time you spend together is precious.
Walking and talking is one of the best things
couples can do for their relationship.

*W*HEN THE IPHONE CAME
on the market several years ago, we were one of the first "kids" on the block to own one. Since we have been Mac users since the 80's, buying one of these babies was a natural thing for us to do. And since both of us love music and both have very eclectic music tastes, the thought of downloading a billion songs gave us chills up and down our respective spines! To date, we have about 9000 songs on our iPhones. Not quite a billion but we are working on it!

Now, you are asking yourself, what does the iPhone have to do with love and marriage? Well, it goes like this. Remember our constant refrain regarding successful loving relationships—"Love is simple to understand. The problem is people won't do the simple things required to make love work." The iPhone is a good example.

We walk a lot and we always take our Wonder Dog, Louie, with us. The many miles we spend walking around our lovely hometown of St. Louis has allowed us to solve most of the problems in the universe! If we could walk more there would be world peace, everybody would have a job, there would be no empty stomachs, and everybody would love each other. Talking and walking is fun and probably has as much to do with our own successful 52-year marriage as anything we do. And our creativity begins to explode on those walks. Everything seems possible. Every problem seems solvable.

Here is where the iPhone comes in.

When we first got our iPhones we started listening to them as we walked. Oh, sure, the exercise was still good and the music was beautiful. The fresh air still smelled the same. But guess what happened—we stopped talking when we walked. It didn't take long for us to realize how much we were missing on our walks. Our creativity began to wane, and for the first time in many years, we began to feel a little tension in our relationship.

Since both of us have worked for a combined 100+ years, we needed those walks together to problem solve and to do the creative thinking required for our books, our research, and our other writings. Those walks were important quality time together. They were so important to our mental health as well. Now, we were messing up all the good things because we were listening to and talking on our iPhones when we were together instead of to each other.

We also began to notice other couples (lovers, friends) with their iPhones in hand as they walked with each other. And they weren't talking to each other, just like we weren't! Something had to be done and we did it—no more walking with each other while listening to our iPhones. No more sitting together in the family room listening to our iPhones. No more listening to our iPhones when were together except when we were on a plane flying somewhere. Since the normal noise on a plane makes it hard to talk anyway, the iPhone shuts out the bad noise and replaces it with beautiful music.

Don't get us wrong—we love our iPhones. We can't imagine being without them. But like most things in life, there is a time and place for everything. The time you spend together is precious.

Walking and talking is one of the best things couples can do for their relationship. Leave the iPhone at home when you share those moments. Save the iPhone for the times you are alone or on a noisy plane. Your relationship and your love will thank you for it.

Those Golden Anniversaries we write about are often achieved as a result of lots of walking and talking! Maybe we will see you on one of those walks. Without the iPhones of course!

Start Living a Meaningful Life

How you live your life matters!
It matters to you and
to the one you love.

*P*HILOSOPHERS THROUGHOUT
history have provided guidance and theories about the importance of living worthwhile lives. But philosophers talk in vast generalities instead of providing helpful lessons that can be modeled.

After hearing yet another speaker philosophically expound about the importance of living a good life without providing any lessons, we were inspired to write this article about the "Ten Lessons of Life and Love." Always remember—inspiration often comes from those you disagree with.

We are pleased to share our "Ten Lessons About Life and Love" with you today. Here they are:

1. ***Each day you wake up, remind yourself of your dreams and the dreams of the one you love.*** It is highly important to have dreams. Dreams remind you of what is important to you, what you value, and what you are motivated to strive for each and every day. A day without a dream is, for most people, a bad day.

   Charley's life experience of growing up poor in a small rural farming community of central Missouri without, as his

Mother used to say, "A pot to pee in or a window to throw it out of," reminds us of the power of a dream! Frankly, we cannot imagine where our lives would be if we didn't have dreams of achieving something far beyond what might have been imaginable to most kids growing up in small towns and in big cities.

2. ***Seek happiness in your life.*** Make your happiness and the happiness of the one you love, a major life goal.

As love and marriage researchers, we have interviewed thousands of successfully married couples in all 50 USA states, 55 countries, 10 Canadian provinces, and on all seven continents of the world over these past 37 years. All these marvelous couples want nothing more than to secure happiness.

Happiness is, in fact, a goal for most people, as it should be. Being happy in life is the goal of rational people. Never forget that!

3. ***Success in life and love has almost nothing to do with luck.*** Our love and marriage work together over these nearly four decades suggests that there is no such thing as luck! Is education luck? Is the development of good moral character luck? Is working three jobs to provide for your family luck? Is marrying the right person luck? Is having a steady job that pays a livable wage luck?

Our answer to these questions is a resounding, NO! To suggest that life is all about luck is to minimize all of the hard work done by folks day in and day out to secure a better future. We have a lot of faith in human beings to work hard to achieve the success they desire. Success has little to do with luck.

4. ***Who you love and want to spend your life with defines who you are as a person.*** Making decisions about whom you want

to love, marry, and spend your life with, speaks volumes about your personhood. Do not make these decisions lightly. People are always defined by what they love. Love well. Love the right person.

Analyze very carefully your decision before you make it, but understand this—loving and marrying the right person might very well be the most important decision you will make in your life. Do not make this decision lightly.

5. ***Good health is, for most people, the secret to a happy life.*** Let's be clear, doing the things that are required for a healthy mind and body are prerequisites to healthy life and love.

As we have written in several books, articles, and blogs over the years, one of the Seven Secrets of a Successful Marriage is this, "long-time successfully married couples care about each other's health and do their best to promote good health in each other. They know that the way you emote, your level of anxiety, your productivity, and your ability to engage in a loving relationship, are all affected by what you put into your mouth (or do not!) and how you maintain the health of your body—both mentally and physically. Successfully married couples long ago recognized that you must manage your mind and mood through food, exercise, and healthy living."

6. ***Every day of your life engage in an act of kindness!*** Be nice to those you meet. Give a compliment or two. Over-tip the waitress or waiter. Wave a person at the supermarket through the cross walk in front of you. Let someone with a smaller cart of groceries go ahead of you in line. Return ugliness from someone with a smile and a "Have a nice day!"

The simple truth is this—people are measured by how they react to adversity, how they react to those who are unkind. It is easy to engage in "road rage." It is far harder to control yourself when offended, chastised, belittled, and treated unfairly. As the British might say, "Stiffen that upper-lip!" Or as our mother's used to say, "It's okay to turn the other cheek."

Life is full of confrontations between nice people and ugly people. Make it your goal to be a good person—a decent person—a nice person. Your life and the lives of those you love will be happier because of it.

7. ***Always be open to diverse points of view.*** Always be willing to listen to and consider a point of view different from your own. Let's face it, it's easy to get angry when someone doesn't agree with us. In modern America, it is increasingly difficult to have civil conversations. Too many people's mantra is, "My way or the highway." Compromise is seemingly a thing of the past.

As Charley's mother used to say, "Life is too short!" What she meant should be clear—if you spend your life arguing about everything—if you spend your life rejecting outright the points of views of others—you will be a miserable human being. Try your best to talk less and listen more to others. It is impossible to hear the messages of others if you do all the talking.

8. ***Don't be a bully!*** The intimidation of others is a bad thing. Respecting those who have less power than you is a good thing. Don't ever be guilty of shouting down another human being. It should be clear—life and love is a lot more fun when you treat others with respect.

Here's the truth—if you don't respect the opinions of the one you purport to love—if you shout down the opinions of others—if you try to bully others into submission—you will ultimately lose in the game of life. Trust us—nobody likes a bully!!

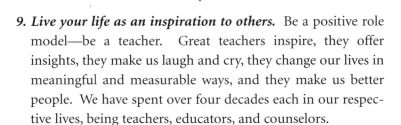

9. *Live your life as an inspiration to others.* Be a positive role model—be a teacher. Great teachers inspire, they offer insights, they make us laugh and cry, they change our lives in meaningful and measurable ways, and they make us better people. We have spent over four decades each in our respective lives, being teachers, educators, and counselors.

At the start of each day of your life dedicate yourself to being a person who wants to inspire others, who offers insights into life, who wants to help others, and who wants to share the knowledge they possess with others. Teachers care. You should care! Share your love, share your knowledge, share "things that matter" in life.

10. *Life is a journey—be engaged.* Charley's mother used to say, "If you woke up this morning you knew it was the start of a good day!" In many ways, life is like a baseball game. There is no clock. The game of life for the most part has no seasons.

One inning of life leads to another and sometimes you win the game, sometimes you lose, sometimes you go into "extra innings." No matter what the outcome, you play the game—for better or worse. In life and love it is important that you play the game—get involved—take advantage of each day of your life. Be engaged in life. Be engaged in love. There is nothing like it.

These are the lessons of life and love. Get engaged today. You won't regret it.

Marriage: The Co-Authoring of Your Life

When you get married, your life is no longer single-authored, it is co-authored.

LET'S GET REAL ABOUT love and marriage—when you get married you are adding a "Co-Author" to YOUR life!

It is clear when it comes to love—marriage is the ultimate commitment. Anyone that thinks getting married is a casual event does not understand the dynamics of love and life. The simple truth is this—when you get married you are adding a co-author for your life. Nothing about your life will ever be the same. And that's a good thing.

Anyone who gets married and doesn't understand that their life will be altered in an unalterable ways, henceforth, doesn't know love—doesn't understand love.

Love and marriage changes everything. Love and marriage changes everything about your love and YOUR life. If you don't understand the ramifications, don't get married. If you want a co-author for your life—get married!

Marriage begins with a lifelong commitment to each other. And the truth is, the element of marriage that so many are unaware of this—when you get married you are no longer writing your own script for life. You are now writing a script of life and love that is "Co-Authored."

We hope you understand the power of co-authorship when it comes to your life—your married life. To think you can get married and continue to write your own life's script is, shall we say, delusional.

For the most part, we write our own script of life after we leave home and the influence of our parents and relatives. We write our own script of life until we fall in love and get married. And then suddenly and without warning, we realize that our life is now being co-authored. We realize that we are no longer in complete control of who we are and who we will become. We are no longer the single architects of our life.

But here is the real deal—married couples wouldn't want it any other way! Having a co-author for your life is a good thing—a positive thing.

Being the "Lone Ranger" in your marriage is not a desired outcome. When you get married, you share the stage. You write history together. You are no longer the complete master of your house. And that is, indeed, a good thing.

The truth is, the most wonderful thing about marriage is that "two become one without losing the individual identities of either." Translated—marriage is a coming together of two uniquely different people who love each other and want to spend their lives together. And once the marriage is consummated, the "co-authoring of your life" begins!

After interviewing thousands of successfully married couples, we have found that successfully married couples learn the synergy and togetherness of turning two-into-one early in their marriages and don't want life to be any other way.

The best qualities of both individuals come together to form a unit of one that is greater than either of the two individuals alone. One couple summed it up by saying, "We are one. We are a team. We support and need each other."

We have found in our nearly four decades of research that those married couples who use pronouns such as "we," "our" and "us" behave more positively toward one another and showed less physiological stress.

The findings of our interviews with thousands of successfully married couples who have been married from 30-77 years, would certainly support these notions. In fact, this "WE" behavior is so critical to great marriages around the world that it is one of the seven pervasive characteristics of successful marriage we have reported in our several books and hundreds of articles.

In successful marriages neither the husband nor the wife dominate the relationship. They have achieved the art of togetherness, without losing their individual identities. They have become, "co-authors" of their life together.

So how did they do it? There are three aspects of turning two-into-one for successful couples.

First, sharing interests, feelings, ideas and memories gives their marriage a uniqueness all its own. Second, compromising to form mutually agreeable decisions that both can support is critically important. And third, the best marriages we have observed thrive on mutual helpfulness and support for each other.

The only way for your marriage to become "WE" instead of "YOU" and "ME" is to put sharing foremost in your relationship. Both partners work to bring out the best in their spouses by enhancing their feelings of confidence and self-worth. They become each other's strongest supporters and routinely think in terms of "WE" and "OUR" and "US."

The more we learn about successful couples achieving true togetherness, the more we are convinced that a great marriage ceases to form if the husband and wife do not attain that feeling of "WE" as a unit of "ONE."

It should seem clear—when you get married, your life is no longer single-authored, it is co-authored. A co-authored life is a good life! Enjoy it as we have for these past 52 years of marriage. Our lives have definitely been co-authored!

How to Build a Love that Lasts

Mastering these twenty-one building blocks
of a great marriage will go a long way
towards building a lasting love.

Successful marriage and loving relationships all require simple, practical acts. Simple gestures. Simple conversations. Success in love and marriage depends upon an accumulation of having done the simple things to construct the foundation for building a love that lasts.

The key ingredients that define a successful marriage are easy to understand, yet difficult for many couples to practice in their relationship. **Here are 21 ways to help you begin Building a Love that Lasts:**

1. ***Be a relationship cheerleader.*** Be the number one cheerleader for your spouse. Support your spouse in every way you can. Let your partner know just how important he or she is to you and to the rest of the world.

2. ***Learn to compromise.*** Compromise is a part of daily living in a marriage. No one can have it all his or her way. Discuss how the two of you make decisions. Establish a plan to work through important issues until you both can find a mutually agreeable solution.

3. ***Share the burdens.*** Carry the burdens of your marriage on four shoulders, not just two. Learn to sense when your spouse needs help, even when they do not ask for it. Helpfulness should become such a matter of habit that you will feel and act like a winning team.

4. ***Communicate constantly.*** Couples must talk about anything and everything. In successful marriage there are no sacred cows—no secrets.

5. ***Leave anger outside the bedroom.*** Never go to bed mad— talk it over first and settle things before sleeping. You may have one very long night before going to bed, but you will get the problem resolved.

6. ***Don't be ruled by emotions.*** Keep your emotions in check when discussing those "sacred cow" issues. These sensitive discussions can be contentious and often heat up quickly. Don't let your emotions interfere with the importance of talking openly about everything.

7. ***Make loving behavior a habit.*** Successful relationships are about mutual love and respect. Habits can be formed either for good or ill, so why not make it a habit to always treat your spouse the way you would want to be treated? Make it a pervasive characteristic of your marriage.

8. ***Respect the individuality of your spouse.*** Your partner is a complex individual with many interests, ideas, desires, habits and experiences. Don't narrowly define your mate's capabilities.

9. ***Do not ever get jealous or angry with your spouse when they need to be alone.*** If they sense your displeasure, they either won't allow themselves the opportunity to be alone or they will resent you for being jealous or angry because of their need to be alone. Remember, the absolute need for privacy

and aloneness is a fundamental predisposition of every human being.

10. *Successfully married couples understand that taking care of themselves in a health sense is not sufficient.* You must also promote the good health of your spouse. To live until "death do us part" requires a mutual concern about good health, including taking proper medications, going to annual physicals, getting proper sleep and exercise.

11. *Use common sense about what you put into your body.* Eat lots of fresh fruits, vegetables and whole grains, while cutting way down on salt, refined sugar, white flour, food preservative, coloring agents, artificial flavoring, hydrogenated fat, nicotine and alcohol.

12. *Smile and laugh together often.* Remember, it takes more muscles to frown than to smile. Save your energy—smile at your spouse instead of frowning. It is the simplest of expressions with the most powerful effects.

13. *It is not your money and my money.* In successful marriage it is OUR money. Be a one checkbook family.

14. *Pay all of your bills together.* That doesn't mean both of you have to actually sit down together to pay the bills. Rather, it means that both of you need to know exactly what the bills are, what is being paid, and what are the outstanding financial commitments.

15. *Never make a major purchase without talking it over with your spouse and then sleeping on it.* You would be surprised at the number of major purchases you don't make if you just sleep on it!

16. *Touching each other multiple times per day is the norm in successful marriages.* Touching says, "I love you so much I simply must touch you." So make a point of touching your spouse in some way at least ten times a day.

17. ***When you go to bed take turns playing the "S" game.*** Have your lover lay on their side with their body shaped like the letter S. Squeeze your body close to theirs by forming an S around them. Enjoy soaking up the warmth and security you feel.

18. ***Use touching as your Morse code to make an exclamation mark of your love.*** Touch your spouse as you compliment what you really like about the way your lover looks. This little habit forces you to pay careful attention to the best qualities of your spouse.

19. ***Successful marriage is exciting, full of unpredictable things, and never boring.*** Don't always do that which is predictable. Upend expectancies. Variety is the spice of life.

20. ***Greet your mate at the door wearing your sexiest looking attire.*** Make it so terrific that no matter what happened to your spouse before they walked through that door, they immediately forget about it. One minor point, make sure it is your spouse before opening the door!

21. ***Send your spouse a love letter or a romantic email.*** Do it when it is least expected, knocking them off their feet with surprise. Taking the time to put into words how much your spouse means to you is the greatest of gifts.

Mastering these 21 building blocks of a great marriage will go a long way towards building a lasting love.

WHAT MAKES LOVE LAST?

IN MARRIAGE SIMPLE THINGS MATTER

Why Do Great Marriages Last for a Lifetime?

Successful marriage represents an accumulation of the reciprocal notion of loving and being loved.

CONTRARY TO THE OPINION of the uninformed, a marriage lasting a lifetime is the norm, not the exception. And the truth of the matter is this—most all successful marriages thrive based upon the relationship between the two people in love, not on other people or extraneous variables.

Recently, we reviewed some research that addressed the issue of how to make the "romance" of a marriage last. While we think the essay generally reflects our research findings, we take issue with some of the reported conclusions.

First, the notion that happy marriages are based on good communication, shared values, a sturdy support system of friends and relatives, happy, stable childhoods, fair quarreling, and dogged determination is mostly true, but not completely true.

Here is what we know—successfully married couples have NOT reported to us that having a sturdy support system of friends and relatives was a prerequisite to their successful marriage. **Quite the contrary, they have reported to us that the strength of their per-**

sonal relationship with each other was based on their relationship with each other, irrespective of their friends and relatives! Imagine that! Having friends and a supportive family is nice, but it is certainly NOT a prerequisite to a blissful, happy, and successful marriage.

And here is the second area where the author has gone wrong— **stable childhoods are NOT a prerequisite to a successful marriage.** We have interviewed couples that have been successfully married for 30-77 years and virtually none of them have reported that a "stable childhood" was the defining element in their successful marriage.

In fact, most of the successfully married couples we have interviewed suggest to us that their childhood experiences didn't matter much with regard to their marriage. Their marriage depended, more than anything else, on their relationship with each other. The success of their marriage was determined by the strength of their relationship with each other, nothing more, nothing less. Let's leave the blame on childhood experiences—for good or bad—behind as unworthy when it comes to a successful marriage.

Now, we move on to the next problem—so-called love blindness, self-deception, or positive illusions. These notions don't hold much water in our humble and well-researched opinion.

Present in the mind's-eye of the most successful marriages we have studied is the simple notion that a person's spouse is eternally beautiful or handsome. And trust us on this, these aspersions of beauty and handsomeness transcend time and place.

The simple and endearing truth is this—would you really expect anything different? To see the one you love in the most positive terms throughout your enduring marriage should come as no surprise to anyone. Having "positive illusions" is not a bad thing—it is not something to ridicule—and it is certainly not something to dismiss as unimportant. "Love blindness" is something to embrace!

Some who study marriage have reported that there is no particular combination of personality traits that leads to sustained romance." Frankly, we find such a conclusion invalid and not supported by our own research. Here's why.

Our research of successfully married couples from different ethnicities, different cultures, different religious traditions, reveals seven personality traits that leads to "sustained romance" and to a successful marriage that transcends time. To suggest that there are no personality traits that lead to sustained romance is to ignore overwhelming evidence to the contrary.

All of this now leads to this inescapable question, why do so-called "experts" report such "findings" as truth when there is so much evidence to the contrary? One only knows!

Here is what we know to be true, there are recurring themes in successful marriages around the world. In a nutshell, they are: togetherness/oneness of the relationship; truthfulness and honesty; mutual respect and kindness; a focus on healthy living and good health; the sharing of important financial decisions; daily tactile communication (frequent touching and intimacy); and surprise and unpredictability (great marriages are never stale or boring). These time-tested relationships speak to the notion of how to make the romance of a marriage last. It really is that simple. Simple things matter in love and marriage. They really work!

As human beings, we have this amazing capacity to love and be loved. In a successful marriage, this notion is multiplied ten-fold! Successful marriage represents an accumulation of the reciprocal notion of loving and being loved.

Predictors of a Successful Marriage

Watch these predictors and odds
are in your favor for a
lifetime of marital happiness.

*I*N OUR SPEECHES AND travels throughout the world we are often asked, "Are there ways to ensure that a marriage will succeed?" The answer is of course, **"no."** Life, love, and marriage do not come with absolute guarantees. Marriage does not come with a warranty.

Let us hasten to add, however, you can greatly increase the odds that your marriage will last for a lifetime if your profile closely resembles the 15 predictors of a successful marriage discovered as a result of our research throughout the world.

The "15 predictors of a successful marriage" are:

1. *It stands to reason that you and the one you love must first pass the Marriage Quiz.* If you can't get out of the starting gate with a successful marriage, the rest doesn't matter. Take the Quiz (you can take the marriage quiz on-line at www.SimpleThingsMatter.com/Marriage_Quiz.html) and if you both receive a score of 18 or higher, you have met the first pre-requisite of a successful marriage.

2. **Wait until you are at least 25+ to get married.** Couples who get married after the age of 25 are far more likely to stay married than those who get married sooner. Experience and wisdom come with age.

3. **Have an income-producing job with stability before you get married.** Here's what we know, couples with annual incomes over $50,000 (vs. under $25,000) experience a drastically reduced risk of divorce.

4. **Do not have children in the first year of your marriage.** Nora Ephron once said, "Having children is like throwing a hand grenade into a marriage!" Children are wonderful, but they bring stress and challenges to a marital relationship, especially to a new marriage. Bring children into the world when your marriage is ready for them.

5. **Being spiritual and/or religious is good for your marriage.** Couples that consider themselves religious or spiritual (vs. not) are considerably less likely to get divorced. Faith and spirituality contribute to the sense of oneness felt by successfully married couples—a necessary prerequisite to a long and happy marriage.

6. **Focus on getting an education that includes post-secondary training.** College educated couples have a much less chance of divorce than those with only a high school diploma. Education almost always leads to enlightenment and understanding and more tolerance for the views of others—so critically important in successful marriages.

7. **Make sure your spouse is your best friend.** When someone asks you who your best friend is, the honest answer must be, "My spouse." There is no other acceptable answer to this question. Being in love is never enough without friendship.

8. *Always fight fair in your marriage.* All married couples argue—the difference is how they argue. Arguing is healthy for a marriage. Just fight fair and never make your arguments personal and hurtful!

9. *Never lose your individual identity or subjugate your individual strengths just because you got married.* While in many ways "two becomes one" in the best marriages, losing the sense of "who you are" hurts your marriage.

10. *Never engage in acts of infidelity.* While some marriages survive infidelity, the overwhelming majority do not. Think long and hard about what you will lose before you engage in infidelity—before you violate the most sacred of marital trusts.

11. *Always allow time to be alone for both you and your spouse.* We have concluded as a result of our research is that every human being has a fundamental predisposition to be alone. Allow yourself time to be alone to your thoughts each day. Extending the same opportunity to your spouse will pay huge dividends for your marriage.

12. *Talk about anything and everything!* Marriages thrive on open communication and honest discussion. The most successfully married couples we have interviewed around the world tell us that they have learned to communicate frequently, fairly, openly, and honestly. Mum is NOT the word in marriages that work!

13. *Always show mutual respect and admiration for each other.* The best marriages repeatedly engage in acts of kindness towards each other with no expectation of something in return. They work hard to understand each other's needs and wants. But remember—these behaviors take daily practice!

14. *The greatest joy in life for both you and your spouse is spending time with each other.* If you do not feel this way, you do NOT fit the profile of the most happily and successfully married couples we have interviewed around the world. There is no substitute for togetherness when it comes to a happily married couple.

15. *Understand that all marriages go through seasons—much like the seasons of nature.* Those marriages that last over time started with the simple planting of a seed. The seed was nourished over time. Love grown with tender and loving care matures into fully-grown love that can withstand the tests of time.

These predictors associated with the best marriages do not occur by accident or happenstance. Heed the advice and the odds are in your favor for a lifetime of marital happiness. Ignore the predictors and do so at your own peril. The choice is yours.

The Core Values of Love

The Core Values of all
successful loving relationships
are at the heart of the matter.

*F*ROM OUR MARITAL RESEARCH,
we have discovered the Seven Core Values of All Loving
Relationships. We have learned much about what makes great
marriages tick—about what makes them successful. Even in spite of
ominous odds from time to time, the best marriages survive and
thrive, and we know why!

Great marriages survive and thrive because both individuals are
committed to the these **Seven Core Values present in all great
marriages and successful loving relationships:**

1. *The couple in love is committed to always putting each other*
   first in their relationship with each other.

   The first thing you notice in all highly successful loving relationships is that those who purport to be in love recognize
   that their relationship is not about you and me, it is about US.
   Discovering that YOU are not the center of the universe is the
   hallmark of a great relationship. Actually putting another
   human being number one is a powerful indication that you
   are truly in love.

2. *The couple in love is committed to democracy in their relationship.*

Always remember, successful loving relationships are egalitarian. Namely, the best relationships understand that theirs is a shared relationship. If one person has all the power and makes all the decisions, it is NOT love! True love is a very democratic thing!

3. *The couple in love is committed to ensuring their mutual happiness.*

Remember, true love is not just about ensuring your happiness. More importantly, and often for the first time in your life, you actually enjoy and are motivated by ensuring the happiness of someone other than yourself. It is a good feeling!

4. *The couple in love values absolute trustworthiness and integrity in their relationship with each other.*

If you cannot trust the one you love, then it is not true love! Trust us on that. The most successful loving relationships report that they trust their mate unequivocally and without hesitation. To violate that trust is to undermine and, ultimately destroy, the relationship with the one you say you love.

5. *The couple in love is committed to caring and unconditional love for each other.*

When you truly love someone you do so without conditions. It is not about loving you IF . . . True love is unconditional.

6. *The couple in love is committed to being mutually respectful towards each other.*

There is a Golden Rule in true love and it is like the one you learned early in your life—"Do unto others as you would have them do unto you." Do not expect to be treated with respect when you are disrespectful to the one you love. Respectfulness is at the heart of all great loving relationships.

7. The couple in love values their mutual sense of responsibility for each other.

People in love care for each other in ways that they have never cared for another human being. They feel a sense of responsibility for another person that they have never felt before. It feels so good to put another's needs above your own. To do so is to love deeply.

The *Seven Core Values* of all successful loving relationships are at the heart of the matter. If you and your mate master these values, your love will, in all probability, last a lifetime.

Do Great Marriages Have a Perfect Life?

The best marriages report the challenges to their marriage ACTUALLY strengthened their marriage.

*W*E HAVE CONSTANTLY and relentlessly pursued this question in our interviews around the world, "Do the great marriages have a perfect life?" And the answer is—absolutely NO!

Too often, people assume that those who have the most successful marriages live in some kind of la-la land—a perfect world—a place where everything is fair, just, and beautiful—a Nirvana land! Here's the truth—nothing could be further from the truth!

From the thousands of successfully married couples we have interviewed there is a most important lesson—even couples with the happiest marriages have experienced severe challenges to their relationship. These couples have reported to us unimaginable challenges to their marriage. Couples have shared with us stories about the death of children, financial burdens that nearly destroyed their relationship, the horrors of losing a job, the burdens of serious health issues, the pressures of child rearing problems and the destruction caused by a transfer to another city for a work assignment that neither of them wanted, to name only a few.

These are couples that have been happily and blissfully married for a long time. These are the couples that know the secrets of a great marriage and a great relationship. The best marriages—the best relationships we have ever witnessed or interviewed—have all reported to us a litany of the great challenges to their marriage throughout their years together.

Ah, but the truth is that the best marriages report the challenges to their marriage ACTUALLY strengthened their marriage and their relationship.

The essence of their story says, "These challenges to our relationship actually made our relationship better!"

So what is the message here? Like all of the most important messages about love and relationships we have learned, the important message is a simple one—challenges make you stronger. And in the end, challenges—properly dealt with together as a team—will make your relationship stronger.

People who have gone through the wars of life together will always choose their mate in battle. People who truly love each other will always say this to us – we are a team and we will always support each in our times of need.

The Good, the bad, and the ugly—dealing with challenges together is the heart of the best relationships.

Never, never assume that the best marriages live in some "Cinderella land." The best marriages have survived heart-wrenching challenges. Never minimize what the best marriages and relationships have gone through.

The challenges they have experienced have made their relationship stronger. Never underestimate the power of challenge to the establishment of a great relationship.

Is Friendship the Ultimate Test of True Love?

No relationship has ever passed the test of time without friendship.

IT TAKES MORE THAN good sex to make a marriage work. Johnny Cash and June Carter had it right when they sang, "We got married in a fever, hotter than a pepper sprout. We've been talkin' 'bout Jackson, ever since the fire went out."

Here's the rub—being "in love" is easy. It's an emotion common to romantic relationships that transcend the millennia. Being in love is definitely central to the best, most successful marriages.

But being in love is NOT enough. No relationship has ever passed the test of time without friendship.

A recent study by Helliwell and Grover backs up this notion of "friendship" as extremely important to marriage. They state, "We find that well-being effects of marriage are about twice as large for those whose spouse is also their best friend."

Frankly, for nearly four decades in our interviews with couples, we've heard—if you do not marry your best friend you are marrying the wrong person. So why is this principle true for all great marriages around the world?

Here are five reasons why partners in great marriages are also best friends:

1. *It's a hard-knock life.* Sharing the burdens of life's challenges and providing each other steadfast support is what best friends do. They shoulder the burdens of their marriage on four shoulders, not just two. Having each other's back becomes such a matter of habit that best friends who marry behave like a winning team in everything they do.

2. *You need a strong advocate.* We all need encouragement to succeed in life. Best friends act as advocates for each other. They support their spouse in every way, providing essential encouragement and that little extra bit of rah-rah-rah (a.k.a. "You can do it!") that helps make good things happen in life for BOTH of them.

3. *Your well-being has an ally.* Numerous research studies show that a positive relationship between the partners in a strong marriage leads to a longer life, with better physical health.

   Married men and women have lower rates of serious illness and are less likely to die in hospitals than unmarried men or women. One study concluded that married men live an average of 10 years longer than unmarried men, and women live an average of 4 years longer than unmarried women.

4. *Communication is open and honest.* In the most successful marriages there are no sacred cows—no secrets. Research indicates that individuals in a healthy marriage feel they always have someone to confide in and lean on in times of need. This support comes from open communication between best friends.

5. *A super-sized portion of trust and loyalty.* Couples who are also best friends literally trust each other completely, with

their lives, their well-being, and their sacred honor. The words successfully married couples use most to describe the one they love include: trustworthy, honest, loyal and truthful.

You see, the standard principle in the most successful marriages around the world is that your partner is your best friend. And couples who claim to "love" each other, but do not "like" each other, are clearly not best friends.

One of the questions of our research interviews is this, "Who is your best friend?" We got a most telling response to the question in Rio de Janeiro. After asking the so-called "Best Couple in Rio" we got answers that drove home this point to us. When we asked the most prominent physician in the magnificent city of Rio who his best friend was, he named ten people and NONE was his wife of 37 years!

And it gets worse—when we asked his wife who her best friend was, she gave ten names and. Like her husband, the list of names did not include him, the prominent physician she had been married to for the same 37 years! They both told us how important their circle of friends were to them, while never mentioning each other.

Here's another good example of our point. When we interviewed a couple in Sydney, Australia a few years ago, as usual, we asked the same question, "Who is your best friend?"

To our surprise, both people in this so-called loving relationship, did not consider each other their best friend. We probed and probed, but alas, neither would admit that their spouse was even one of their closest friends.

The simple truth of the matter is this—these two couples professed to "love" each other, but they did not "like" each other. They were clearly not best friends. In fact, when we asked clarifying questions, it became quite clear that neither couple had friendship within their respective relationships.

Make no mistake about it—loving someone is NOT enough. If they are not your best friend, your relationship with them will not pass the test of time. Your relationship with them can never be judged as a great success.

If the one you love is not your best friend, your relationship in all likelihood, will not become one of the lifelong love stories we have heard throughout the world. But if your partner IS your best friend, congratulations. And remember, never take them or their friendship for granted.

The Foundation of Love Is Trust

*Being honest and trustworthy
is at the heart of all the best
loving relationships we have studied.*

SUCCESSFULLY MARRIED COUPLES never cheat on their spouse! To be truly in love is to be unequivocally and unconditionally dedicated to the one you love. To betray your spouse in intimate ways is to destroy your relationship, make no mistake about that. Most marriages cannot recover from this form of betrayal. Don't fool yourself into thinking it can.

When conducting our interviews with successfully married couples we are always profoundly struck by their undying trust in each other. They literally trust each other with their lives, their well-being, and their sacred honor. The words they use to describe the one they love, more often than not, include words and expressions like trust, honesty, loyalty, respects me, admires me, always there for me, never lets me down, truthful, and never lies to me. Their trust for each other is about as complete as you can get. And when we ask couples in love during our interviews to place, in an overall sense, where their relationship is on a 10-point scale with 10 being "Absolute Trust," without exception, they say "10!" Isn't that wonderful? Remarkable? These are the couples that will celebrate their golden anniversaries together!

Trust is not something all loving relationships start with. For some couples the trust becomes complete in a few years. For others, it takes awhile. But one thing is for sure, happy and successful marriages and relationships survive and thrive on the basis of this trust. Trust is so pervasive in their relationship that they never give it a second thought. They expect it. It's always there. It is part of the fabric of their relationship.

There is one thing you can take to the bank—all people in love have faced temptations in their relationship. The pretty girl in the restaurant captures your fancy. The handsome man walking down the street draws your attention. The flirt at work is tempting at times. And, we will dare say, sometimes in every relationship you think about slipping in the sack with some of the beautiful people you meet. But here's where it stops—these are only fleeting moments of passing fancy. These are the moments of momentary lust for another human being that are not acted on.

Why? People in love who are happy in their relationships control their urges because they know that while a moment of sexual fantasy is healthy and normal, following through and enjoying sexual satisfaction with someone other than their mate— cheating on their mate—is destructive to the loving and trusting relationship between them. It's okay to have sexual urges and fantasies regarding another person, but to act on them ruins all that trust. It destroys the tie that binds.

Couples who are truly in love in their relationship know that a few moments of sexual satisfaction can NEVER replace the loving, trusting, and caring relationship they have developed with their mate. As someone once said to us, "I have a marriage license but I didn't give up my looking license!" Admiring others in intimate ways is normal and healthy. But acting on those urges has ruined many a marriage and many a loving relationship.

Those wonderful couples we have interviewed resist these normal urges and temptations of life because they know their relationship is so much more important to them. Destroying the trust between them causes the foundation of their relationship to crumble.

Character in a successful marriage or relationship does matter, and character is about trust. Being honest and trustworthy is at the heart of all the best loving relationships we have studied. It really is a 10 on a 10-point scale. In our estimation, character is the foundation of true love!

The foundation of true love is trust. Destroy that foundation and you destroy your love. When you do so there is rarely redemption—there is rarely ever reconciliation. Never forget this simple truth—there is character in the best loving relationships. Practice good character and your love will not only survive, it will thrive.

The Loving Touch

It is their way of saying
"I love you so much
I simply must touch you."

WE'VE BEEN MARRIED FOR 52 years and simply can't keep our hands off of each other! For many years, we thought we were unique. Then we started our research for our book, and did we get a big surprise—virtually every happily married couple we interviewed reported the same condition! Over time we have come to call it the "tactile response." Literally translated, it means, "I touch you here, I touch you there, I touch you everywhere!"

During our interviews with married couples we pay a lot of attention to their tactile interactions. More often than not, they sit on the couch during the interview and hold hands or place some part of their body on their mate's body. It is their way of saying "I love you so much I simply must touch you." So why all of this touching?

As part of our interviews we asked the couples to tell us what they believe to be the most endearing and important characteristics of their spouse. We continued with the following questions: "How would you describe your spouse? What adjectives would you use?"

Here are the words we most often heard: encouraging, positive, loving, honest, has integrity, beautiful (or handsome), understanding, wonderful, patient, loves life, loves me, unselfish, giving, caring, trusting, generous, helpful, conscientious, and humorous. Words to live by in a marriage, wouldn't you say? And they said these things unabashedly, without apologies.

Successful couples know nearly everything about each other. They have studied in infinite detail how their spouse looks, feels and acts. They know what makes the one they love tick and can recite in scripture and verse their best qualities. They brag about each other all the time. They love each other for a whole bunch of reasons and don't mind telling you what they are.

What do their words about each other have to do with touching? Here's what we observed during our many interviews—when couples told us something special about their spouse in response to our questions, they would touch each other as if to emphasize the importance of the words. Touching was like an exclamation mark! Over time, we believe that these couples, like the two of us, say these words with a touch, without always saying the words out loud. Touching becomes kind of a *Morse Code*—a substitute for language and the expression of feeling. Successfully married couples have mastered the *Morse Code* of marriage—it's called touching.

A wise person once said that if you pass your spouse 100 times a day, you should touch them 100 times a day. When you touch someone, you are acknowledging his or her presence and expressing your love. In effect you are saying, "I love you so much I simply must touch you.

Is Successful Marriage Ageless?

Familiarity and intimacy with someone
you purport to love is one
of the greatest joys on Earth.

RECENTLY, ABC News-Denver reported the story of a World War II veteran in tears after receiving "a long-lost love letter he wrote to his future-wife when he was at war in Europe 70 years ago." The letter was recently discovered inside of an old record bought at a thrift store.

Ninety-year old World War II Veteran, Bill Moore's beloved, Bernadean, died in 2010. Mr. Moore was quoted as saying, "But I loved her, and she loved me. That's all I can tell you. It's a heartache not being with her all the time."

Their daughter was quoted as saying, "Their love sets such a beautiful example of what life can be."

In our many travels around the world conducting our marriage research, we are often ask this question, "Is Successful Love and Marriage Ageless?" The answer is, YES! Here's why.

Successful marriages and relationships, like fine wine, do get better with age. **There are many reasons why, but following are a few of the most significant and important ones.**

Reason #1 – Imagine spending 30 or more years with someone! You know everything about them. You know their strengths, their weaknesses, their hot buttons, their failings, their likes and dislikes, and their deepest and darkest secrets.

When you are in this kind of relationship with someone you are, more than likely, more intimately connected to this person than anyone on Earth! And honestly, can you imagine a better place to be with another human being? We think not, and our research around the world supports this simple notion—familiarity does not breed contempt amongst people who deeply love each other. Familiarity and intimacy with someone you purport to love is one of the greatest joys on Earth according to those successfully married couples we have interviewed who have been married for 30-77 years.

Reason 2 – The most happy and successfully married couples report to us that there is no one they would rather spend time with than their spouse. There should be nothing mysterious about this finding. The longer you are married, the more you get comfortable being with the one you love.

Reason 3 – Can you imagine preparing and eating most of your daily meals with one person for 30+ years? The truth is, there are a lot of people out there in the real world, across continents and cultures, who have been married for more than three decades of life, and whose daily rituals include garnering their daily sustenance in the presence of the same person. When you break daily bread with someone for most of a lifetime, there is one undeniable fact—you love that person, you cannot imagine life without them, and you find that sharing meals with them is a necessary and highly important part of your day. Marriage does improve with age. Our research would suggest that there is no denying that.

Reason 4 – There is one undeniable truth of life—spending your life with someone you love makes you much more happy than

spending it alone. Our research around the world reveals a number of significant truths, but none more important than this—loving someone completely and intimately over the adult life span is one of the greatest gifts of life. Long time successfully married couples around the world report that they cannot imagine life without their spouse. Spending time WITH their spouse is much more rewarding than spending their time alone.

Reason 5 – And finally, and perhaps most importantly, the longer successfully married couples are married, the more likely they are to get toxic people out of their lives. The longer you are married they more likely you are to avoid people who make you unhappy and who give you stress. Many of the couples we have interviewed tell us this—life is too short to have it poisoned by people who don't really care for you, who don't share your likes and dislikes, and who make you unhappy.

The best marriages learn the most important lesson of life— don't surround yourself with people who don't love you and who don't share your value system. Life is, indeed, too short. Spend your time wisely.

You see, there really are important life lessons to be learned as you travel through time with someone you love. Those lessons will sustain your love, they will nourish you love, and they will ensure a love that will last a lifetime. Learn these lessons today. Those who have been successfully married for much of a lifetime understand. We hope you will as well.

Hopefully, your love affair will, like the Moore's, set an example of what life and love can be.

Successful love and marriage is, indeed, ageless.

Can You Have a Great Marriage Without Great Sex?

If you think anybody's marriage is going to last 30 or more years just because they have good sex—well, forget it! It isn't going to happen.

OLDER ADULTS BETWEEN THE ages of 57 and 85 make sex an important part of their lives! That's the results of the first comprehensive national survey of the sexual attitudes and behaviors of older adults as reported in the *New England Journal of Medicine*. And, as you might have guessed, our 37 years of research with successfully married couples found the same conclusions.

For sure, nearly every happily married couple we have interviewed reported at least a reasonable degree of satisfaction with their sex life. But you know what, NOT ONE of the couples we interviewed who had been married 30-77 years reported that their sex life was central to overall success of their relationship. Not one! Sure it was important, but if you think anybody's marriage is going to last 30 or more years just because they have good sex—well, forget it! It isn't going to happen.

Lasting marriages are characterized by frequent moments of intimacy and bliss. Over the years, we have had a wonderfully healthy sexual relationship with each other. Sometimes our sex is so good . . . . . well, we won't bore you with the details!

We could wax on and on about the role of sex in a marriage, but others have done that over and over. Those who write about sex all the time might have contributed to much of the dysfunctionality surrounding sex in relationships. Frankly, some popular books we have seen on the subject hold up a standard of sexual performance and gratification that hardly any couple could achieve. And worse yet, couples that can't live up to the "standard" think they've failed. Many times their relationship suffers.

For starters, we all know that good sex can be fun, romantic, exciting, and something that makes most consenting adults feel warm and fuzzy all over. Over the years we have interviewed thousands of successfully married couples, and most report a reasonable degree of satisfaction with their sex life. But here is our most important research finding concerning this issue, no marriage was ever made successful because the couple had a great sex life!

And more importantly, when we ask successfully married couples how important sex is to the success of their marriage—to rank on a scale of 1-10 with 10 high—the average rank was only 6! This finding has held true over the more than 30 years of our research. The results are hardly a resounding endorsement for the importance of sex in a successful marriage.

You see, marriage is a multi-faceted and highly complex relationship, and in the best marriages no one aspect stands out as the make or break part of it. The truth is, there are seven pervasive characteristics present in all successful marriages. And guess what, sex is not one of them! Sex is only part of one of the seven characteristics of a successful marriage.

As we say so often in our many interviews and writings, all of the married couples, representing the best marriages we have interviewed, have shared with us the importance of touching in their relationship. One gentleman we interviewed told us that if he passed his wife in the house a hundred times a day, he touched her. To touch someone you love is to acknowledge their presence and to communicate your love for them. That's why the most successfully married couples amongst us do it so often.

We believe that the overemphasis on sex on television, in the media and in books about marriage cause people to believe that if they don't have stupendous sex everyday there is something wrong with their marriage. Marriages that fail do so for a variety of reasons and not for a single reason. Simply put, our research findings hold true that no marriage was ever saved or made successful because the couple had a great sex life!

We have reported many first hand accounts from successfully married couples who tell us how important the human touch is to a loving marriage. They hug each other often, the kiss, they touch each other while talking, they sit cheek to cheek on the couch while having a conversation, they curl around each other when they sleep or just gaze at the stars, and yes, they have sex from time to time— when it's right for them.

You see, people touch each other in many, many different ways and no single form of touching wins the day. It's what we like to call "the accumulation of touching" that matters. Touch the one you love often and in whatever way your heart desires. It's that human connection that wins the day—and wins the marriage! The simple truth is, the best marriages engage in a lot of touching, sex is only one form of touching.

Our message should be clear to our readers—in successful marriages sex can be fun, important, and a healthy way of being intimate with your partner. Just because you get older and have been married for 30 years or more does not mean that your sexual life has to be less active. On the other hand, based on our research and first-hand experience, we think it is grossly overemphasized in terms of its centrality to successful and long-term marriages. So much more is present in those relationships that pass the test of time. Sex is only one of them and is certainly not the most important for couples with long lasting successful marriages.

As the study in the *New England Journal of Medicine* points out, the sexual activity of older adults is not as much tied to their age as it is to their physical health. In the next chapter entitled, *Eat, Drink, and Exercise Your Way To a Great Marriage,* we talk about how successfully married couples focus on each other's physical health. So, even though sex is not central to the overall success of your marriage, we would like to leave you with this final thought—if you would like to continue enjoying sex into your later years, take time today to focus on the physical health of both you and the one you love.

Eat, Drink and Exercise Your Way to a Great Marriage

*Frankly, and in our humble opinion,
we have a mutual responsibility
to each other to do our
best to maintain our health.*

OW THAT WE HAVE YOUR ATTENTION . . .

We completed our annual physical examinations today. Long ago we established the tradition of scheduling our respective annual physicals on the same day. Why, you ask? It's simple really—we love each other from the bottom of our respective hearts and want to be around each other for as much as we can for as long as we can.

Think about it—beyond your own health whose health do you concern yourself with the most? We bet it is the one you love the most. In the loving relationships we have observed over the years, including our own, we note how much happier people are in their lives when they are personally healthy and when the one they love the most is healthy as well.

Frankly, and in our humble opinion, we have a mutual responsibility to each other to do our best to maintain our health. We eat well, take our vitamins, are religious about taking our medications every day, and riding our bikes on the many trails in St. Louis has become nearly addictive. We encourage each other to do all of these things and then top off our year by having our annual physicals. It is always better to catch a health problem in the very early stages so a physical exam is a must. Oh, and the good news is—we passed our physicals with flying colors!

Doing our best to stay healthy for ourselves and for the ones we love is the best way we can think of to say, "I love you." And being healthy makes that "physical love" all the more fun and exciting!

The couples we have interviewed around the world who have great marriages know the importance of being healthy in BOTH a physical AND mental sense. Research says you can eat, drink and exercise your way to a great marriage.

Unless you have been living in a hole for the past 50 years, you know that proper nutrition is essential for good PHYSICAL health. No one disputes this simple notion. Make no mistake about it—what we eat, drink, and otherwise ingest into our bodies has a significant effect on both our physical and mental health.

Why do so many believe that proper nutrition only applies to good physical health and not to good mental health? What could nutrition possibly have to do with good mental health and a great marriage? Plato said it best, "If the head and the body are to be well, you must begin by curing the soul."

According to the *Diagnostic and Statistical Manual of Mental Disorders* (DSM-V), ". . .4 out of the 10 leading causes of disability in the US and other developed countries are mental disorders. Major depression, bipolar disorder, schizophrenia, and obsessive-compulsive disorder (OCD) are among the most common mental disorders that currently plague numerous countries and have varying incidence rates." Many scientists believe that the root causes of several of these diseases are nutritionally based.

Studies show that a lack of certain dietary nutrients contributes to the development of mental and associated disorders. For example, essential vitamins such as vitamin C and the B vitamins, certain minerals, and the omega-3 fatty acids, have been found to be deficient in patients suffering from mental disorders, including depression. Unfortunately, these vitamins are often deficient in the general population in America and other developed countries.

A number of years ago, Charley taught a special seminar course entitled, "Nutrition and Mental Health." He admitted a half-dozen, carefully selected graduate students, and they began a journey to discover the truth about the relationship between mental health and proper nutrition.

They collected data for a good part of a semester from a myriad of international sources. They then compared their findings about mental health and nutrition to selected scales of the well-known and much used Minnesota Multiphasic Personality Inventory (MMPI).

To the astonishment of Charley and his students, the correlation between nutrition and mental health was overwhelming. They took their results and created what they called the "Psycho-Nutrition Inventory" (PNI, 1983).

The simple truth they discovered was that the single best predictor of selected scale scores on the MMPI was the PNI. *Translation—the best predictor of mental health was nutritional intake, or lack thereof!*

Imagine the surprise and joy over this important discovery! The best predictor of mental health was a score on an inventory that measured nutritional levels! Does the word "breakthrough" come to mind?

To quote from Charley's study in 1983 (which still holds true today):

"Namely, there is a sufficient amount of evidence available in the Orthomolecular research literature to suggest that a maladjusted person is certainly not going to get better psychologically if he/she continues to exhibit nutritionally maladaptive behaviors. Clearly, if maladjusted clients can learn to effectively control those nutritional and corollary habits that increase their mental "unhealthiness" as defined by psycho/ nutrition theory, then they at least have a fighting chance to become healthy through the utilization of other treatment strategies employed by the counselor."

In order to sustain a quality relationship with the one you love you need to have good mental health. In order to maintain good mental health you need to engage in proper nutrition. That means you need to eat healthy and engage in healthy activities! Virtually all of the "rules" you hear about healthy eating and healthy living for a healthy "physical body" also apply to a healthy "mental body." The elixir of good health is exercise, healthy eating, and nutritional supplementation to fill in the holes.

As we have written about in our several books, articles, and blogs over the years, one of the *"Seven Secrets of a Successful Marriage"* is this—long-time successfully married couples care about each other's health and do their best to promote good health in each other. They know that the way you emote, your anxiety, your productivity, and your ability to engage in a loving relationship, are all affected by what you put into your mouth (or do not!) and how you maintain the health of your body—both mentally and physically. Successful marriages long ago recognized that you must manage your mind and mood through food, exercise, and healthy living.

The Shocking Secret to a Happy Marriage— Alone Time

*The recognition and practice of the
absolute need for privacy and aloneness is,
in our judgment after analyzing thousands of
interviews, a fundamental predisposition
of successful marriages.*

STOP THE PRESSES!
We have discovered the most important ingredient of a successful marriage! And you know what it is? The answer is . . . drum roll, please . . . allowing time for those who inhabit the relationship to be alone!

Successfully married couples around the world over our past 37 years of interviews have told us this very simple truth during our interviews with—the secret to their successful marriage is having time to be all to themselves—to their own thoughts, their own meditations, their own self, and their own physical space.

Isn't this an interesting notion? In the best marital relationships between a man and a woman, having time alone tops the chart of what makes their marriage work. You can take this advice to the bank!

We have heard this expression, or some variation of it, over and over during our travels and interviews on the world's seven continents. The amazing consistency of the stories we have heard about aloneness have surprised us on the one hand, but have assured us on the other. Here's why.

This is what we have learned to be true—the most important ingredient of a successful marriage is to be content with yourself. Only those who are capable and willing to spend time alone can be described as content with themselves.

This contentment with self is so very important to a successful marriage. What we have learned from these successfully married couples is this—if you can't live in your own skin, it is difficult to share yourself with someone else. Being content with oneself is the pre-requisite to engaging in a healthy, happy, and successful relationship with another human being.

There are many lessons to be learned from this notion of aloneness in a successful marriage, but the most essential are:

1. *The most important pre-requisite to a successful relationship with another person is this—being content with yourself.* Learn to live within your own skin. Liking you comes first. Liking yourself allows for the development of positive relationships with others. Work on this notion as if your marriage depended on it!

2. *Respecting your own need for privacy and aloneness is an important first step in building a loving relationship with your spouse.* There is a fundamental predisposition of every human being to have time alone. Recognizing and understanding that need in yourself and your spouse is a huge step towards building a love that lasts.

3. *Aloneness is not a bad word!* Spending time alone is good for everyone. Not recognizing this need can be highly detrimen-

tal to your relationship with the one you love. Learn this lesson well. If you never give yourself or the one you love time to be alone, you do so at the detriment of your relationship.

4. **Too many failed marriages report to us this fact with alarming consistency—their spouse would not give them time to be alone to themselves.** When we probed the meaning of all this they reported to us one important finding, "My spouse suffocates me!" The meaning of suffocation in a nutshell—I had no time to my own thoughts, my own being, and my own feelings. My spouse did not respect my need nor their own, to be alone. The suffocation destroyed our marriage!

5. **We feel assured that the need to be alone is a "universal truth."** Successfully and happily married couples around the world have reported this "truth" to us repeatedly and overtly. This notion is not an American thing. It is not a European thing. It is not an Asian thing. The secret ingredient for the best marriages around the world is to respect the need for privacy and aloneness in yourself and in the one you love. Never forget it! All successful marriages are built on this foundation. Give your life's partner the priceless gift of privacy and aloneness.

We have witnessed from time and time again marriages in which one or both partners failed to understand the importance of being alone, not only for themselves, but for their spouse as well. When we first introduce this concept to others, the reaction is usually one of surprise. Many couples are of the mistaken notion that they are to be constantly attentive to their spouse. While their intentions are good, their desire to be attentive causes them to, in fact, interfere with the quality of their communicative relationship with their mate. The desire for too much closeness can inadvertently drive a wedge between husband and wife. Isn't that ironic?

In all probability, many couples believe that quantity of time together is the most important characteristic of their relationship. Instead, the "law of diminishing returns" comes into play here. The economists would explain it something like this. Let's say you buy a case of your favorite cola and decide to drink it in one setting. The first cola tastes great. Perhaps the first two or three taste good. But after about four or five, the quality of taste begins to diminish. If you were to drink the whole case in one setting, you would like each cola less and less until you reached a point where you began to absolutely hate your favorite cola. The "law of diminishing returns" seems to appropriately describe many marriages doesn't it? More is not always better. Give your spouse some privacy . . . the opportunity to be alone. Expect the same opportunity for yourself. Don't allow communication in your marriage to fall victim to the "law of diminishing returns."

In our interviews, we have been continuously reminded of the importance of privacy and aloneness to the success of a marriage. The recognition and practice of the absolute need for privacy and aloneness is, in our judgment after analyzing thousands of interviews, a fundamental predisposition of successful marriages. The amount of time available to satisfy these two needs varies from one marriage to another and from one marriage partner to another. But one thing is clear, all marriages will stand the test of time only if these duel needs are recognized and respected. How do you and your spouse improve the quality of communication based on this notion?

Each individual has a different level of need that can change at different stages in their life. Understanding and recognizing the level of need can be quite difficult at times, especially for a person with a low level of need for privacy and aloneness. Being alone to your thoughts provides for you a periodic psychological renewal. A few moments alone to your thoughts each day frees the spirit and cleanses the soul. Do not deny yourself these moments together with yourself. You know what we are talking about don't you? Remember, to recognize that your spouse also has these same needs.

Just as important is assuring yourself and your spouse that it is natural to have this need and that everyone has this need. In other words, feeling guilty about needing and wanting alone time is not appropriate or healthy. Recognize the need and embrace it.

If you and your spouse allow each other time for privacy and aloneness, think of the possibilities. The quality of communication can only be enhanced between the two of you after refreshing your mind and spirit with alone time. Did you ever notice how hard it is to talk and listen to someone else when your mind is overflowing with thoughts about work, home, children, and the like? No matter how hard you try, you listen but you do not really hear. And you want to know why? It is because you have denied yourself those moments of belonging only to yourself. What kind of real communication goes on between the two people in a marriage within this context? We believe the evidence is clear—not much!

Isn't it interesting that at the root of successful communication with your mate is no communication at all? You'll have to admit, this is an interesting notion with considerable merit. While we were quite taken with the idea in our early interviews with successful couples, it was not until some of their stories and examples so poignantly illustrated the concept that we fully grasped the importance of the need for privacy and aloneness to respect. Sometimes we try so hard to be great communicators that we end up with results opposite of our intentions. Because of our social nature, we have been misled into believing that we must always socialize. You only have to consider this for a moment to see the fallacy in this kind of thinking.

If we were pressed, we would probably admit that privacy and aloneness have been at the top of our list of needs many times in our marriage. We live such hectic lives at work that the time to be alone with our own thoughts is paramount to our engaging in any meaningful communication with each other. The recognition and respect for these dual needs are fundamental to successful communication in a marriage. If we are unable to communicate, nothing else matters.

You have to belong to yourself before you can belong to others. Do not miss the opportunity. As the song goes, "Even lovers need a holiday . . . time away . . . from each other!"

How to Keep
Your Marriage Vibrant

*The simple truth is, sometimes
we need to fall in love
with our spouse all over again!*

*E*VERY SO OFTEN,
a marriage needs to "strike another match" and rekindle the flames
of love. The simple truth is, sometimes we need to fall in love with
our spouse all over again!

When your marriage starts to stagnate, when it starts to suffer
from the doldrums, and when it needs resuscitation, rest assured,
there are five actions you can take to bring your marriage back:

1. ***The human touch is paramount to the most basic of all
   human connections.*** So, the first thing you must do in re-
   establishing the passion of your relationship is to touch!
   Touch often. Touch much. Hold hands when you walk. Take
   turns wrapping around each other in bed at night. Feel the
   warmth. Feel the love. If you pass your spouse 100 times a
   day, touch them 100 times. By touching you are acknowledging their presence and telling them how much you love them.
   Get started today!

2. ***Engage in a process that allows you to re-establish the communication links between the two of you.*** We suggest that

you start with these three questions: 1. Why did we fall in love? 2. Why did we get married? 3. What are our hopes and dreams for the future? The communicative links between the two of you are highly important and no love, no marriage, and no relationship will ever be jump-started again without the re-establishment of the communicative ties that bind. Try getting started with programs like our "Seven-Week Program for Developing Ongoing Sharing in Your Marriage" in *Building a Love that Lasts: The Seven Surprising Secrets of Successful Marriage.*

3. ***Work hard to have fun with each other!*** Dine out at your favorite restaurant. Spend a night in a motel. Take a vacation to Disneyland, just the two of you! Cook a romantic dinner at home. Whatever you do, do something that ignites the passion and the fun! Do something that takes your relationship "beyond boring" and makes your lives exciting and fun-filled. Rediscover what makes you excited, what gives you a sense of adventure, and what makes your adrenalin flow! Successful marriages are not boring! Plan a passion starter today!

4. ***Upend expectancies!*** Do not always do that which is predictable. Here's an example. One of the lovely couples we interviewed a few years ago told this wonderful story. Their life together was getting too predictable and too boring. At 85 years of age, they were both entirely too focused on "settling in." But as they shared with us, it didn't have to be that way. When Clarence came home one glorious Sunday afternoon, he was met by his beautiful wife, Grace, at the front door in her "altogether." Grace thought, "What the heck, if I can't get him interested in anything but golf and TV, I will just meet him at the door naked." As it turns out, Clarence got the message. Of course, what happened after this homecoming

episode they didn't share with us! But, they sure did upend expectancies.

5. ***Tell your spouse how much you love them and why!*** Never, we repeat, never, fall into the trap that says, "I don't have to tell him/her I love them, he/she knows I do." Nothing could be further from the truth! Never take the one you love for granted. Big mistake! To love someone is wonderful. To tell them you love them is amongst the greatest gifts you could ever give.

You see, the rekindling of love is not so complicated. Doing these five simple actions can re-ignite your love affair with your mate.

Seven Simple Ways to Make Your Love Last

Great marriages require much work on a daily basis to build habits of positive interactions and mutual support.

*F*ALLING IN LOVE IS EASY, but making love last takes work. Success in love and marriage depends upon an accumulation of having done the simple things to construct the foundation for a lifetime of love.

Yet, doing the simple things is difficult for many couples to put into practice in their everyday relationship. **Here are seven simple ways to make your love last:**

1. Become the number one cheerleader for your spouse. Support your spouse in every way that you can. Let your partner know just how important they are to you and to the rest of the world. Perhaps the best help that you can give your spouse is to give them the confidence they need to become all that they can be in everything that they endeavor to do. Be your spouse's strongest supporter. Become their cheerleader. Remember that when your spouse reaches the top of the mountain, you will be standing there with them.

2. ***Learn how to use compromise as part of daily living in your marriage.*** No one can have it all his or her way. We share the bed, the toothpaste, the car, the house, and the bills. While this sounds so simple, it can cause some unusual challenges as the two individuals in a marriage have to discuss and work out mutually agreeable arrangements for such minor issues as who uses the shower first and who takes out the trash, as well as major issues such as where to live, if children will be a part of the family, and what car to purchase. Discuss how the two of you will make decisions. When you share a marriage, you must learn the art of compromise—giving a little to gain a lot.

3. ***Act like a winning team by making helpfulness a matter of habit.*** Carry the burdens of your marriage on four shoulders, not just two. Both of you individually are good, but the two of you working together can be a dynamite team. The old saying that two heads are better than one is very true in a marriage. Ideas that the two of you generate can be better than most ideas generated alone. As you begin working together you will learn to sense when your spouse needs help, even when they do not ask for it. You will have a "sixth sense" that tells you when your spouse is in need. Sharing life's burdens on four shoulders is certainly easier than on just two.

4. ***Communicate constantly.*** Couples must talk about anything and everything. In successful marriage there are no sacred cows—no secrets. The same is true of your relationship right now. Build those communication skill between the two of you right early in your relationship.

5. ***Leave anger outside the bedroom.*** Never go to bed mad—talk it over first and settle things before sleeping. You may have one very long night before going to bed, but you will get the problem resolved. While this is the number one piece of

advice from the thousands of happily married couples we have interviewed throughout the world, it is also true for your relationship right now. Don't part ways angry. Solve the problem before you leave each other.

6. *Use touching as your Morse code to make an exclamation mark of your love.* Touch your loved one as you compliment what you really like about the way your lover looks. This little habit forces you to pay careful attention to the best qualities of the one you love.

7. *A successful relationship is exciting, full of unpredictable things, and never boring.* Don't always do that which is predictable. Upend expectancies. Variety is the spice of life. Bring that excitement into your relationship everyday.

These seven tips will help you enhance the relationship with the one you love. You will begin forming a habit of taking positive actions to build your love for a lifetime together.

None of the successful couples we have interviewed throughout the world have said that their relationship was easy and everything was always fine. Great marriages require much work on a daily basis to build habits of positive interactions and mutual support, but the benefits you will gain from a lifetime of successful marriage are tremendous.

Successfully married couples report the importance they feel of always being able to count on their spouse for moral support when they are down in the dumps. This comes from the togetherness they have established in their everyday interactions with each other.

Never Go to Bed
Mad at Each Other

Do not be fooled by those who tell you that it is not important to resolve divisive issues before you go to bed.

ON THE *TODAY SHOW* a remarkable segment aired. It was remarkable not because it was good or enlightening, but because it wasn't. In fact, it was downright misleading and irresponsible based upon the research evidence, and we want to comment on it.

A psychologist and the managing editor of a well-known magazine were on a television show to proclaim that the notion of "never go to bed mad at each other" was a myth. Imagine, calling such a time-honored notion a myth. Listening to them made our skin crawl and here's why—credible research does not support what they said.

We have learned a lot about what makes good marriages work interviewing thousands of successfully married couples. Towards the end of our interview protocol we ask these wonderful couples if they could offer three pieces of advice that we could share with newlyweds. And guess what, the number one piece of advice they have given, and it is has been consistent over the years, is "Never go to bed mad at each other!"

Remember, this advice comes from happily married couples. The advice they give isn't designed to shock the media with something unusual or out of the ordinary. These are the words of couples with a proven track record. Frankly, we got the impression when we watched the interview with the psychologist, that the purpose of referring to "Never go to bed mad at each other" as a myth was to get a spot on a highly watched morning television show! But the sad truth is, their message was a terrible message to send to newly married couples. Our fear—they just might listen to the advice they heard on TV and that would be a big mistake in our judgment.

From time to time you hear so-called experts throw out information as if it were scientific fact. People believe it as if it were gospel. The problem is, much of what you hear has no scientific or research base.

The good news about the notion of "Never go to bed mad at each other"—it is based on research from those who would know best—those who have been happily, blissfully, and successfully married for 30-77 years! The lessons learned from *thousands of combined years of successful marriage* speak for themselves.

Married couples do, from time to time, have disagreements. They argue over big things and little things. They argue over stuff that doesn't matter and stuff that does. But here is what we have learned from our research—successfully married couples rarely ever go to bed without resolving their differences on an issue, be it big or small. Many report to us that they have stayed up all night trying to bring closure to an issue that has divided them. They know that gaining resolution is far more important than getting a good night's sleep. And remember this, issues that are not attended to more often than not fester through the night and only appear worse in the morning.

Do not be fooled by those who tell you that it is not important to resolve divisive issues before you go to bed. They are simply misguided and the advice they give can be hurtful to your relationship. Accept the advice of those who know—those whose marriages are happy and have stood the test of time.

Myths, No-No's and Misconceptions About Marriage

Successfully married couples practice truth and ignore the mythologies.

*K*NOWING THE difference between myths and facts about marriage can improve your chances for success. For example, it is a fact that if you get married before the age of 24 in the USA, you have a MUCH higher chance of getting divorced than those who get married at 25 and beyond. In fact, *the divorce rate for those getting married after the age of 25 is only about 30%*—less than half the divorce rate for those getting married before the age of 24!

The facts about marriage reveal that people who get married older, who have higher education levels, who do not have children when they get married, and who marry someone of their general social class, have a much higher chance of marital success than those who do not meet these thresholds. In the end, what really matters are the truths about marriage, not the mythologies about marriage.

Here are the Top Ten Mythologies and Realities about Marriage based on our marriage research:

Mythology #1 – Married couples have sex lives that are less satisfying than those who are not married. *REALITY* – Not true! In fact, the research evidence supports the opposite conclusion—those who are married have far better sex lives and enjoy it more than those who are not married. There is no debate in reputable circles about this fact!

Mythology #2 – Cohabitation works as well as marriage. *REALITY* – Those who cohabitate are not as committed to their relationship as those who are married. In fact, those who cohabitate before marriage have a significantly higher divorce rate when married than those who have not cohabitated!

Mythology #3 – Married women have a higher risk of domestic violence in their marriage than unmarried women. *REALITY* – Simply not true!! In fact, women who are married have a far LESS chance of being abused than those who cohabitate without being married.

Mythology #4 – Marriage can survive infidelity. *REALITY* – While some marriages do in fact survive infidelity, the overwhelming majority do not. Think long and hard about what you will lose before you engage in infidelity.

Mythology #5 – The more educated a women is the less likely she is to get married. *REALITY* – There is no basis in fact for this mythology. In fact, college educated women are more likely to get married than their less educated counterparts.

Mythology #6 – Bringing children into a marriage strengthens the marriage. *REALITY* – Nora Ephron once said, "Having children is like throwing a hand grenade into a marriage!" Children are wonderful, but they bring stress and challenges to a marital relationship. Be prepared for the ups and downs!

Mythology #7 – When you get married you lose your individual identity for the benefit of the oneness of your marriage. *REALITY* – Nothing could be further from the truth. In the best marriages neither spouse loses their individual identity or subjugates their individual strengths.

Mythology #8 – The one you are married to does not have to be your best friend. *REALITY* – Our four decades of research across cultures and continents reveals the opposite. In fact, the most successfully married couples report to us in our interviews with them that their best friend in life IS their spouse.

Mythology #9 – There are no particular advantages to being married. *REALITY* – In our own research and in the research of others, there are clear advantages and benefits to being married including living longer, being healthier, and accumulating more wealth. The health benefits accrue more to men and the financial benefits more to women.

Mythology #10 – The most successfully married couples don't argue. *REALITY* – Absolutely not true! In fact, all couples argue – those married successfully and those who are not. The difference is how they argue. The best marriages fight fair. If you decide to submerge your feelings, let the anger fester, and go to bed mad at each other—well, you are heading down a path that could ultimately lead to the destruction of your marriage. Arguing is healthy for a marriage. Just fight fair!

The truth of the matter is this—the best marriages survive and thrive—many for a lifetime. And those successful marriages know the differences between truth and mythology. They practice truth and ignore the mythologies.

Based on our extensive worldwide research, we have concluded that these are the four marriage no-no's that really aren't all that bad:

No-No #1 - Wanting some time alone away from your spouse is not necessarily a bad thing. In a successful marriage there are times when you just want to be alone. The absolute need for privacy and aloneness is a fundamental predisposition of every human being. That means having time to be all to yourself—to your own thoughts, your own meditations, your own self, and your own physical space. Too many failed marriages report with alarming consistency—their spouse would not give them time to be alone to themselves and they felt "suffocated." Having time alone is not really a no-no.

No-No #2. - Asking for some individual attention from your wife when she is too focused on the kids is not really a marriage no-no. Married couples often report that they wish their spouse would pay more attention to them than to the kids. Even in a successful marriage, children add stress to a relationship because of the added demands on time and attention. When a mother or father focuses too much on the needs of the children in lieu of paying attention to their spouse, it will most assuredly be detrimental to their marriage. The quality of the relationship between husband and wife trumps everything else! Get it right and good things follow. Get it wrong and lots of bad things often happen!

No-No #3. - It is not always bad to comment on your spouse's weight gain. Most married couples want to be proud of the way their spouse looks. When excessive weight gain changes their spouse's appearance, many find it hard to deal with. It is more than just appearances—it is also about health issues related to excessive weight gain. Successfully married couples understand that taking care of each other in a health sense is not sufficient. You must also promote the good health of your spouse. To live until "death do us part" requires a mutual concern about good health, including taking proper medications, going to annual physicals, getting proper sleep and exercise.

No-No #4. - Wanting to actually hear "I love you" from your spouse is a natural desire, not a bad thing. Truth is, we have learned many things from the thousands of couples we have interviewed. But, the most pervasive theme in all of their interviews is that people in love say so! They tell each other every day. They shout it to the stars each day. To be in love—to be truly in love—is to tell your spouse that you love him every day of your life. We often hear, "Oh, I don't need to tell her, she knows I love her." Wrong! If you love her you must tell her everyday how much you love her and how important she is in your life.

Too many people look for the idealized version of love. Idealized love rarely happens. You will only be disappointed if you believe "idealized love" can describe your love.

When you fall in love, it is important to understand that being in love is the easy part. The rest takes hard work. And because of this, our greatest challenge as researchers is to convince those falling in love that the Cinderella story is only the beginning of love, not the end.

The truth is, the Cinderella version of love rarely ever happens. Somewhere along the way, someone forgot to tell those who think they are in love that life isn't always fair, just, and beautiful all the time. Sometimes, the reality of love and the "Cinderella of love" are not the same.

The importance of understanding these 14 misconceptions and realities about marriage will go a long way in helping you build a lasting love with your spouse:

Misconception #1. - Everyday of our marriage will look like a Hollywood romance novel with glittery events and romance at every turn. **REALITY** – A small percentage of your time together will actually involve romance. You will still have to take out the trash, pay the bills and clean the house.

Misconception #2. - We'll have SEX every night. **REALITY** – Johnny Cash and June Carter said it best, "We got married in a fever, hotter than a pepper sprout. We've been talkin' about Jackson ever since the fire went out." Passion cannot compete with real life and intimacy won't happen every night.

Misconception #3. - There will be a "Magic Genie" who cleans your house. **REALITY** – You and your spouse will have to divide up the routine responsibilities that are required to make things work.

Misconception #4. - We have plenty of income, so we will live happily ever after. **REALITY** – Even if you happen to be in an upper income level when you get married, there is no guarantee that your income will remain high, that both of you will keep your jobs, that you will not have to move to keep a job, or that one of you will not face serious health issues effecting your employment later on in life.

Misconception #5. - We have always had good luck so we will be lucky in marriage. **REALITY** – Luck has very little to do with a successful marriage. Rather, a successful marriage takes hard work and commitment to make love last for a lifetime.

Misconception #6. - Love is all we need because our love is so passionate and strong. **REALITY** – Friendship, support, respect and trust are collectively what makes for a strong love, that intensifies over a lifetime together. While passionate love is great, it is not enough to sustain a relationship over a lifetime.

Misconception #7. - Since I am a self-sufficient person, our marriage will be easy because I don't have to depend upon my spouse for support. ***REALITY*** – Everyone needs someone to lean on. Being a Lone Ranger does not work in a marriage. One of the greatest benefits of being married is the support and encouragement each individual gets from their spouse.

Misconception #8. - We will be even closer when we have kids. ***REALITY*** – Happily married couples report that while children are a joy they also bring stress and tension to the relationship. Nora Ephron said it best, "Having a first child is like throwing a hand grenade into a marriage.

Misconception #9. - My spouse will always know what I am thinking. ***REALITY*** – Your spouse will not know what you are thinking unless you tell him or her what you like, what you dislike, or what you want to do for fun over the weekend. When you lash out at them they will not know that you are angry about work, and not them. They will not know you love them unless you tell them! This misguided guarantee can lead to a great many disappointments.

Misconception #10. - Everyday will be a "Mastercard Adventure" in some exotic place, doing exciting things. ***REALITY*** – While that may occur from time to time, that is rarely the norm.

Misconception #11. - Now that we are married, we will always be happy. ***REALITY*** – You have to find happiness within yourself before you can be happy in a marriage. A successful marriage requires both inhabitants of the marriage to be happy. It is not an either/or proposition.

Misconception #12. - Now that I am married I will no longer be lonely. ***REALITY*** – Marriage can be a marvelous friendship and a lifelong relationship, but you, yourself, will have to join in to make it a friendship without loneliness. Loneliness will not just magically happen.

Misconception #13. - Now that we are married, I will get everything I want in life. ***REALITY*** – No one in a marriage gets everything they want. A marriage is about compromise and finding satisfaction in life together.

Misconception #14. - If you are married for 30 or more years, you will have a happy marriage. ***REALITY*** – Only couples who work at their relationship and achieve a satisfying relationship together will be happy. Just being married for 30 or more years does not make you happy. Love is not about longevity! True love has a higher standard.

As you can see, there are many myths, no-no's, and misconceptions about successful marriage. To learn and understand them all is a necessary first step in building a successful marriage and a love that lasts.

WHAT ARE THE WARNING SIGNS OF TROUBLE?

IN MARRIAGE SIMPLE THINGS MATTER

An Unhappy Marriage
Can Kill You!

*Research reveals that a bad marriage
has many deleterious effects on the
heart and a person's overall health.*

O VER THE YEARS,
we have reported ad nauseum the many health benefits of a good
marriage.

There is nothing mysterious about the correlation between a
great marriage and good health. In our humble opinion, this conclusion is a no-brainer—and study after study reinforces this
notion.

And wouldn't you know, a recent study out of the University of
Michigan and the University of Chicago adds support for the thesis
that *a good marriage is good for your health.*

It came as no surprise to us that noted researcher Linda Waite
was one of the principle researchers in this most important study
out of the University of Chicago and Michigan State University, two
highly respected research universities.

Professor Waite, a notable researcher about marriage for several
decades, and Michigan State's Hui Liu, looked at five years of data

about 1000 married folks who participated in a study about social life, health, and aging. The couples studied ranged in age from 57-85.

Their conclusion—"these results show that marital quality is just as important at older ages, even when the couple has been married 40 or 50 years."

Moreover, they concluded that a bad marriage has many deleterious effects on the heart and a person's overall health.

The simple truth is this—a good marriage is good for your heart and a bad marriage is bad for your heart. It doesn't get any simpler than that!

So, friends, what are the benefits of a good marriage? Following are some of the most important. Make note of these benefits. You will be glad you did.

The health benefits of marriage (physical and emotional) have been well documented since the 1850's when a British epidemiologist by the name of William Farr concluded that the unmarried die "in undue proportion" to those who are married. He offered, "The single individual is more likely to be wrecked on his voyage than the lives joined together in matrimony." We would offer that his conclusions still apply today.

Dr. Edward P. Ehlinger, commissioner of the Minnesota Department of Health, concluded the following in an article dated September 22, 2012: "Recent studies confirm Farr's observation of lower mortality rates and better physical and mental health among married individuals. Married men and women have lower rates of depression, Alzheimer's disease, cardiovascular disease, smoking, substance abuse and cancer. After controlling for other factors, married couples have higher levels of cognitive functioning, happiness and life satisfaction. All the health benefits of marriage are consistent across age, race and education groups."

His conclusion is powerful and totally consistent with our own research findings. Married folks are healthier, happier, more mentally well adjusted, more socially adjusted, better off economically, and have healthier hearts!

There should be nothing surprising or Earth-shattering about these notions. It stands to reason that those who have somebody—"Everybody needs somebody, sometime."—will be happier, healthier, and more socially well adjusted.

Human beings are social animals—they want and need someone to spend their life with. When they have someone, they are, in fact, healthier—on virtually all fronts. Why would anyone argue against something so obvious? Why would anyone deny such a well-known truth? In our estimation, it is clear that the best marriages understand the health benefits of marriage. To deny these benefits is to bury your head in the sand.

So why how does being married translate into important health benefits? Simple, really. People who are married help take care of each other's health and here is how they do it.

Recognize that the health of you and your spouse is critical to your relationship, both short-term and long-term. Successfully married couples watch out for each other's eating habits, exercise, vitamins, and medicines because they know that their relationship with each other is enhanced when they are healthy. If you get married young, there is a tendency to ignore the health risk factors because you think you will live forever. Instead, begin thinking long-term and focus on developing healthy habits both physically and mentally.

These seven actions regarding the healthy living habits of happily married couples explain why they live longer:

1. Learn to cook healthy meals together. Enjoy each other's company while you spend extra time communicating with each other. Find recipes that are fun to fix and fun to eat together. A good way to start is to try a few of the salad recipes we have included in our book, *Building a Love that Lasts* (Jossey-Bass/Wiley, 2010). They are from happily married couples all over the world who realize that healthy eating benefitted their relationship with each other.

2. ***Develop a regular exercise program together.*** It doesn't matter if it is just walking together in the evening after work or riding bicycles in the park or going to the gym or swimming. What matters is that you do it together and commit to staying on a regular program to enhance your physical and mental health. Yes, exercise does make a positive impact on your mental health.

3. ***Focus on maintaining good psychological health for yourself and your spouse.*** Having a shoulder to cry on or someone to lean on when things get tough can keep you from the depths of depression. Life can throw unbelievable challenges in your path, so having your spouse as your best friend can provide both of you with the support you need to make it through the tough times together. Like the song goes, "that's what friends are for."

4. ***Take a balanced regimen of vitamins and other nutritional supplements.*** Don't fool yourself into believing that you will get all of your nutrition by eating a well balanced diet. While it might help, with the stress in today's life it is critical that you make sure that you get the required vitamins and minerals with a good vitamin supplement.

5. ***Eliminate bad habits.*** In other words, cut back on your foods containing refined sugars, white flour, salt, food additives such as food coloring, artificial flavorings and preservatives. Stop smoking. Limit your intact of alcohol to 1-2 drinks per day. Get off the couch—exercise. Get more consistent sleep.

6. *Get regular annual medical check-ups.* Encourage your spouse to get a regular physical check-up annually by scheduling your appointments on the same day. Preventative care is far superior to having to deal with a health issue that went undetected for a long period of time.

7. *Make living a healthy well-balanced life a priority.* Just like everything else in life, you have to set your goals and priorities focused on what is important to you. While you may not have any health issues yet, if you develop healthy living habits that focus on maintaining a healthy well-balanced life style, you have a far greater chance of celebrating your golden years together.

You see, the health benefits of marriage come about as a result of the relationship between two people in love. It does take two to tango. Marriage has many health benefits because of the behaviors of those who entered into the sacred bond of marriage. Honestly, does this surprise you?

There are many health benefits of marriage. Take advantage of them. You won't regret it.

Love well. Love healthy. Live longer!

Seven Warning Signs Your Marriage Is in Trouble

It is important to recognize the telltale signs of a failing marriage and determine if they are evident in your relationship.

*T*HERE IS NOTHING more painful than watching your marriage disintegrate before your eyes. It hurts. In fact, it may be amongst the most painful experiences you will have in your lifetime.

During our many radio and television interviews over the years we are often asked this simple question, "How will I know if my marriage is in trouble?" **Our research with couples around the world has identified seven warning signs your marriage is in trouble:**

1. One or both of you show increasing disrespect for each other.

In failing marriages, there are growing signs of disrespect. Resentment and contempt have replaced patience and love. You go out of your way to avoid being together.

And sadly, when you are away from your spouse you are happier than when you are with them. Having fun with your mate seems to be a thing of the past. When mutual respect and understanding fail, your marriage is well on the way to its end. Make no mistake about that.

2. You fight and argue much more often than before and do so unfairly.

Fact is, you have nothing nice to say to or about each other anymore. You love to nitpick at each other. Your teasing isn't fun, it is now painful and hurtful. You use each other as a personal pincushion!

Sadly, your arguments are repeatedly about the same subjects. You are increasingly critical of each other, you fight constantly, and you no longer fight fair. As we have said many times before—it is okay to argue—all successfully married couples do—but the truth is this, successfully married couples have learned how to fight fair. Their arguments do not become personal and attack oriented.

3. You and your spouse are no longer capable of communicating with each other in meaningful and productive ways.

Communication between a husband and a wife is of paramount importance to the health of a successful marital relationship. Failing marriages communicate less and less. There are fewer and fewer meaningful exchanges between the two people who occupy the marriage bond.

Worse yet, they don't talk with each other about their mutual problems anymore. Frankly, failing marriages lose the ability and the willingness to resolve their marital problems. They just don't care anymore. When communication between a husband and wife shuts down, there is little hope for the marriage. Always remember this, no problem was ever resolved, no divide ever bridged, and no disagreement ever broached when people refused to communicate. When communication falters, a marriage is in trouble.

4. Sexual intimacy in your marriage is low and increasingly non-existent.

In a failing marriage, sexual intimacy is low. Sexual intimacy becomes more and more infrequent. Marriage partners turn into roommates, they live together in the same home, but do not share the intimacies of a marriage. Unfortunately, intimacy becomes a thing of the past.

It is clear from our marriage research that sexual intimacy is over-rated when it comes to the best marriages. There are many other elements that are equally or more important to a successful marriage than sex. But make no mistake about it; INTIMACY is more than good sex. Intimacy is holding hands on a walk, snuggling in the morning, hugging a lot, touching each other, and in general, feeling emotion for each other.

5. *Your conversations and discussions are dominated by financial arguments.*

It is clear, when you argue increasingly and incessantly about financial issues, your marriage is in trouble. We have written extensively about this subject over the past few years, and if the truth were known, most arguments in a marriage center on financial issues.

Worse yet, you discover your spouse is lying about money and other financial related issues. They lie about the bills, the balances, the payoffs, and the commitments. A very bad sign, indeed.

From time to time marriages experience trying times when it comes to finances. But the truth is that the best marriages survive and thrive during trying economic times. The best marriages find a way to deal with the economic uncertainties. Failing marriages have not learned to cope with economic uncertainty because they have not learned how to communicate with each other about marital finances. If all you talk about is your financial plight, you marriage is in trouble.

6. *Your spouse cannot be trusted anymore.*

Trust is the centerpiece of a great marriage! In fact, there is nothing more central to a successful marriage than the ability to trust. If you can't trust your spouse, whom can you trust?

When you or your spouse start to have thoughts of being unfaithful and think more and more about divorce, your marriage is in trouble. Let's face it, when the trust level between you and your spouse nears zero, there is little hope for your marriage.

7. *Family members increasingly choose up sides instead of striving for common ground and common understandings.*

Your immediate family find it more and more difficult to find common ground in debates, discussions, and conversations. Family members start to choose up sides. Winning and losing becomes the order of the day. Compromise is out the window.

Moreover, you and your spouse try to isolate each other from family and friends. Divide and conquer becomes the order of the day.

It is sad but true, those marriages that become dysfunctional display symptoms of division and lack of common under-standings among family members. Family unity begins to disintegrate. Feuding families are not good for a healthy marriage.

It is important to recognize the telltale signs of a failing marriage and determine if they are evident in your relationship. When you witness the signs, take action. Save your relationship if you can. Having a healthy and happy marriage is one of the great success stories of life. It is not too late to save your marriage.

How to Kill Communication in Your Marriage

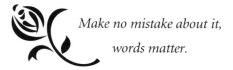

Make no mistake about it, words matter.

NEGATIVE AND HURTFUL statements can have the power to cut through the very fabric of the bond between two people in love. Words can damage and potentially destroy the foundation of your relationship. Make no mistake about it, words matter.

While we have learned many lessons over the years from our research with thousands of happily married couples, one of the most profound is about the importance of the words in our relationships.

The advice from these great couples about **the five things you should NEVER say to your spouse** once again demonstrates why these couples are role models for all who want to stay happily married:

1. *I told you so!* Trust us on this—these four words are rarely ever used in successful marriages. This kind of "comeuppance" has no place in a loving relationship. There is no need to remind your spouse that you were right about something and they were wrong. Talk about wasted criticism!

2. **It's your fault!** Sometimes, a financial decision goes bad, one of your children gets in trouble at school, or some household calamity occurs. And know this—things do go bad from time to time in any relationship. Decisions turn out wrong. Stuff happens! But the blame game never works! It alienates. It divides. It most certainly undermines trust and openness in your relationship.

3. **Why do you always . . .** Focusing on your spouse's weaknesses rather than building on their strengths will only increase their weaknesses and diminish their strengths. This habit can send a relationship into a downward spiral if weaknesses are pointed out and commented upon. Success does breed success. Stick with the strengths and don't focus on the weakness.

4. **Saying "I am mad at you about . . . "** in a public setting. Criticizing your spouse in public or to someone else can do permanent damage to the trust in your relationship. True or not—it doesn't matter. Keep private things private.

5. **Seriously?** Talk about a conversation stopper. "Seriously" is an automatic put-down. It assumes that you think your partner is wrong and instantly puts them in their place.

Since saying negative or hurtful things can be damaging to a loving relationship, it is wise to take extra caution before engaging your mouth when these negative thoughts come to your mind.

Here are four questions to ask yourself before you speak:

1. **Will my comment hurt?** Sometimes we just blurt out things that are hurtful or negative without thinking about their impact.

2. **Am I just mad and need to wait before I speak?** When you are mad is not a good time to judge whether a statement will have long-lasting negative impact. Just be silent for a moment

to determine if you are acting reasonably or if you are too mad to judge the damage you will invoke by your statement.

3. **Is it worth it?** There is so much long-term damage that can be caused by negative or hurtful comments that it really has to be a critically important issue to take that type of risk.

4. **Could I say it a different way?** Many times a negative or hurtful statement can be said in a positive manner. Often with a bit of time to reflect it will become apparent that there really was no need to make the statement at all.

All too often people forget that one negative or hurtful statement can undo an entire day's positive actions and words, damaging the very core of the relationship. So, be mindful to choose words that will enhance your relationship each and every day.

Nine Things Your Husband Isn't Telling You

Even in the best marital relationships, there are things that men think about but don't tell their wives.

*E*VER ASK YOUR HUSBAND what he is thinking and not get an answer? Even in the best marital relationships, there are things that men think about but don't tell their wives. Our interviews with successfully married couples around the world, revealed nine important things that men don't share with their wives on a regular basis.

Here are the nine things your husband might not be telling you but wish you understood:

1. *There are times when I just want to be alone.* Men need time to be all to themselves—to their own thoughts, their own meditations, their own self, and to have their own physical space. Not recognizing this need can be highly detrimental to your relationship with the man you love.

2. *I really wish you would pay more attention to me then to the kids.* Children add stress to a relationship because of the constant demands on your time and attention. The quality of the relationship between husband and wife trumps every-

thing else! Get it right and good things follow. Get it wrong and lots of bad things often happen!

3. **Even though I never say anything about it, your weight gain bothers me.** A man wants to be proud of the way his wife looks. When excessive weight gain changes his wife's appearance, many men find it hard to deal with. It is more than just appearances—it is also about the health issues related to excessive weight gain.

4. **I really wish you would tell me more often that you love me.** To be in love—to truly in love—is to tell your spouse that you love him every day of your life.

5. **I wish you would just say it instead of giving me subtle cues.** Men have difficulty picking up on emotions and subtleties, so they hate it when you hint. A man wants his wife to be direct and say what is on her mind about her feelings.

6. **I worry about not being able to perform sexually, especially as I age.** It is important to a man that his wife makes him feel confident and successful in his sexual relationship. A man needs his wife to help him relax and just enjoy the love they share.

7. **Your constant criticism and corrections really make me feel terrible.** Even though women want to fix their mate, it can have devastating effects when the focus is on the problems and not on his strengths.

8. **I want to be praised, appreciated and validated.** A man needs to be recognized for who he is, what he does and the contributions he makes to the family. He does not want to be taken for granted and have his efforts go unnoticed.

9. **I wish my wife would hug me, caress me, touch me often, and be more intimate with me.** I need her frequent touching to acknowledge my presence and importance to her.

If you haven't had an honest discussion with your husband about these issues, make a commitment to begin that conversation today. If your husband has a tendency to keep issues to himself instead of sharing, it can lead to dissatisfaction with your relationship.

Ten Things Your Wife Isn't Telling You

*Your marriage could be a lot happier
if you figure out what
your wife isn't telling you.*

VEN IN THE BEST marital relationships there are things left unsaid. Our interviews with couples around the world, reveal ten important things that wives don't often share with their husbands on a regular basis, but they should:

1. **There are times when I want my husband's undivided attention**—no TV, no iPhone, no computer—nothing but me!

2. **It is important to me that my husband help with daily tasks** like doing the dishes, cleaning the laundry, setting the dinner table, changing a diaper, helping clean the house. I want my husband to help me out even if he works outside the home and more importantly, if we both do.

3. **I want my husband to communicate with me openly and honestly,** even if it means his telling me things I don't want to hear!

4. **Sometimes I feel exhausted, overwhelmed, inadequate, sick, hurting, and in need of a break** from all things household-

focused. Too often when he asks me how I'm doing, I tell him, "I'm fine" even when I am not! I wish I could tell him more often how I really feel.

5. *I wish my husband would hug me, caress me, touch me often, and be more intimate with me.* I need his frequent acknowledgement of my presence and my importance to him.

6. *I wish my husband would text me, email me, leave sticky love notes for me, write me poetry or love letters*—any positive way to make me feel valued, loved, and respected. I want to feel like I am his priority!

7. *My husband needs to listen more to me when I express my feelings, my desires, my uncertainties, and my fears.* I need a space where I can be imperfect, a place where I can express my feelings without filtering. I need permission to be imperfect.

8. *Sometimes our marriage is all work and no play.* I want to tell my husband to be more fun, not monotonous, and to be more exciting. Occasionally upending expectancies in our relationship would be a good thing. Doing something exciting from time to time would help our marriage move "beyond boring."

9. *I want my husband to recognize me for what I do.* I don't want to be taken for granted and my efforts to go unnoticed. He needs to express his gratitude of me more often for the many contributions I make to the family.

10. *I want my husband to listen to my problems, not try to solve them for me.* I need a good ear, a sounding board, and the like, but I do not need or want for him to tell me what I should think or do!

If you haven't had an honest discussion with your wife about these issues, you need to make a commitment to begin that conver-

sation today. If your wife has a tendency to keep issues to herself instead of sharing, it can lead to dissatisfaction with your relationship.

If there are things on this list that you are talking about with your husband, don't be silent anymore. The better he understands what you need, the better your chance of being satisfied. Don't be guilty of not telling your husband what he needs to hear from you!

Seventeen Fool-Proof
Ways to
Destroy Your Marriage

*Avoid doing these seventeen proven
marriage killers if you want to have
a long and happy marriage.*

*T*HE KEY INGREDIENTS that define a failed marriage are easy to understand and, unfortunately, too many couples unwittingly practice these failed practices every day of their relationship with each other.

Here are seventeen research-based and time-proven ways you can absolutely cause your marriage to fail. Pay close attention to the following and if you do, we guarantee that your marriage will fail.

1. *Always bring anger into the bedroom.* Always go to bed mad at each other! Never talk it over first and settle things before sleeping. Why resolve the problem that confronts you before you go to bed. It can wait until the morning!

2. *Rarely communicate directly with each other.* Never talk about important marital matters. You have lots of secrets to keep from each other! Taking the time to put into words how much your spouse means to you is just a waste of time.

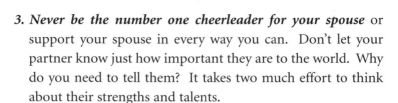

3. *Never be the number one cheerleader for your spouse* or support your spouse in every way you can. Don't let your partner know just how important they are to the world. Why do you need to tell them? It takes two much effort to think about their strengths and talents.

4. *Never make loving behavior a continuous action on your part.* Habits can be formed either for good or bad, so make it a habit to never show your spouse love, kindness or caring. Your spouse will surely respond in kind.

5. *It is best to NOT let your spouse know you are thinking about them.* Don't call them during the day, don't text them, never send a romantic email or leave a love note on their wallet or purse in the morning or on their pillow at night. Increasing the positive communications between the two of you is not necessary for your relationship.

6. *Don't make a point of touching your spouse in some way multiple times a day.* Touching says to most happily married couples, "I love you so much I simply must touch you." If you want your marriage to fail, avoid touching at all costs.

7. *Always do that which is predictable—never engage in something exciting and new each day.* Why bother making it a point to do something stimulating to keep your love for each other vibrant and alive. Get into the relationship doldrums.

8. *Focus on the negative with at least one negative or sarcastic action directed towards the one you love each day.* Don't get them a cup of coffee. Don't ask about how their day went at work. Your spouse does NOT need you to do something nice for them each day.

9. *Infidelity is okay and it is forgivable!* Go ahead and cheat on your spouse. They'll forgive you, right? The heart of all great marriages is trust, but that doesn't matter in your case. Go ahead and engage in a behavior that has destroyed marriages for the millennia. You'll be the exception, right?

10. ***Married couples should commit to always putting themselves first in their relationship with each other.*** Understand that you are the center of the universe. Why put your spouse first. Waste of time, huh? Why bother to attend to their needs since your needs are the only ones that count.

11. ***Democracy in your relationship is dead.*** Let's face it—only one of you is in charge of your relationship, so it might as well be you. The theory that you are the one who rules in your relationship is guaranteed to destroy your marriage.

12. ***Married folks should first and foremost ensure their individual happiness at the expense of their spouse.*** The only person that matters in your relationship is YOU! Really, isn't happiness all about you? Don't worry about your mate. Happiness comes to the selfish.

13. ***No need to value absolute trustworthiness and integrity in your relationship with each other.*** Lying and cheating are AOK in your marriage. Always remember, trust in failed marriages is just a word, not a commitment.

14. ***Never commit to caring and unconditional love for your spouse.*** Always make your love come with conditions. I will love you IF. I will support you IF. I will respect you IF. That action defies everything we know about successful marital relationships, but, hey, you are the exception right?

15. ***A couple in love never needs to be mutually respectful towards each other.*** Air the dirty laundry of your marriage in public. Call your spouse names in public if you are of a mind to. Treat them like a dummy. After all, your mate hasn't earned your respect. Let it all hang out! What's the harm?

16. **You don't have to value the mutual sense of responsibility for each other.** Heck, your marriage is all about you, right? You are responsible about YOU, not your spouse. Don't worry about the health and wellbeing of your spouse. It's their problem. What do you owe them? Being selfish and self-centered is a virtue in a successful marriage, right?

17. **And finally, always remember this—never discuss your financial matters with each other.** After all, it is your money and my money and never the twain shall meet. Spend your marital money freely, irrespective of your financial ability to do so. When you want to buy something, go ahead. Why should it matter whether your spouse will concur? Why should it matter to you that the major cause of marital discord centers on financial matters!

The truth is, it is so easy to fail at your marriage. If you engage in or practice any or all of the aforementioned activities, your marriage has a good chance of failing and it will be your fault.

Can You Save Your Marriage?

Most marriages can and should be saved – but not all!

M OST MARRIAGES AND relationships are worth saving and can be saved, but not all!" Marriages involving sexual, physical or mental abuse are simply not worth saving. In fact, to attempt to save them puts one or both partners in the relationship at risk for further abuse.

Do you know how hard this fact is to accept for people like us— the eternal optimists who always see a pot of gold at the end of the rainbow—who always see a silver lining? Unfortunately, the truth is the truth when it comes to love, marriage and life itself.

Our decades of research on the topics of love and marriage, tell us that some relationships become so poisoned, so dysfunctional, and so hopeless, that it is better to end them than to operate under the illusion that they are worth saving or can be saved.

We recently interviewed a young American couple that had been married for 15 years. It was clear from the beginning of the interview that this was not a match made in heaven. In fact, this marriage had failed so miserably that the only just and decent thing to do was end it. End it now! No amount of counseling and therapy, no amount of praying, and no amount of hoping were going to save this marriage.

The husband in this relationship had "mentally abused" his wife for their entire marriage. He discounted her every word. He made her feel insignificant by his words, his deeds, and by his actions. And even though his wife was pursuing a doctoral degree at one of America's most prestigious universities, he treated her like she was some kind of dumb cluck—someone capable of nothing significant, lasting, or meaningful.

When we interviewed them, it became clear to us that she had had enough. She had had enough of his disrespect, his belittling, his mental abuse, and his coldness. She had finally decided that if she were to have any life at all, their marriage and their relationship would have to become history. So, she decided to end it.

The truth is, the mental anguish she suffered over the years had taken its toll – on her, her three children, and on her marital relationship. She asked us the most profound question of all—"How can I continue to live with a man that makes me feel so worthless, so insignificant, and so meaningless. How can I continue to live with a man that respects me so little?"

Her questions reveal the truth of all this. Sometimes it is just best to move on. Sometimes, to save your soul you have to free yourself of all that is oppressive. Sometimes, you must remove the albatross around your neck if you have any hope of living out your life with happiness, hope, self-respect, and meaningfulness.

Sometimes, you simply must move on with your life before it is too late. For the couple we interviewed, her time had come. The action she must take was clear. The action she must take to save her soul and the souls of her three children became clear to her—if she had any hope at all for her life and her children's life, the time to move on was now!

The simple truth is, some marriages and relationships should not and cannot be saved. As harsh and evident as this truth is, it cannot be avoided in the case of some marriages and relationships.

And in the end, when you have exhausted the solutions available to you, you simply must cut the tithes that bind.

Most marriages can and should be saved—but not all! When you can look in the mirror and honestly and truthfully say that you did your best to save your relationship with another human being, but to no avail, then ending it is the right thing to do. Life is too short to waste it in torment, in abuse, and in lost love.

Save yourself.

One Approach to Fixing Your Marriage that Might Actually Work

"Upstream" therapists always work to help you and your partner create a good marriage.

*I*F YOU'RE CONSIDERING marriage counseling, it's important to know that counseling methods come in two basic modes—what we call the "upstream approach" and the "downstream approach." Let's illustrate with a story.

A marriage counselor is fishing in the Missouri River. Every 30 minutes or so, the counselor hears a voice from the water shouting, "Help me, help me. I'm drowning!"

The counselor throws down their fishing pole on each occasion, swims out into the river, and saves the drowning person. This episode happens over and over for several hours. Then, it happens again.

At about the time of the next "drowning," along comes a second marriage counselor. The second marriage counselor keeps on walking upstream, to the astonishment of the first marriage counselor who, indignantly asks, "Why aren't you helping me save this drowning person?"

To which the second counselor replies, "No, I am going upstream to find out who is pushing all these people in!"

There you have it—two distinctly different approaches to marriage counseling.

The old saying, "An ounce of prevention is worth a pound of cure" applies here. It is better to keep a marriage from getting into trouble in the first place than trying to fix it after the problems are full-blown and the life of the relationship is in true jeopardy.

There are, of course, various approaches to saving a marriage in trouble. But, we believe an upstream approach to building a strong marriage works FAR better that the downstream approaches that often fail. Why?

Because your efforts should center around learning the best way to create and sustain a good marriage versus fixing a bad or broken one.

So, as you seek support for your relationship, find a counselor who believes in working with a couple before they're drowning in the depth of their problems

"Upstream" therapists always work to help you and your partner create a good marriage with deep love and positive interpersonal communication. Do your best to get it right in the first place (upstream) rather than trying to invest all your energies in fixing your marriage later (downstream).

Both personally and professionally, we know a great deal about what it takes to keep a successful marriage thriving. As such, we aren't naive enough to believe there is no merit to both counseling approaches, but working hard to build a love that lasts goes a long way toward ensuring marital and relationship success. Upstream is better! Go for it!

What to Look for in a Marriage Counselor

It is critical to find marriage advice
from a counselor who exhibits
seven characteristics necessary
for effective counseling.

ACCORDING TO THE
National Center for Health Statistics, there were approximately 2.25 million marriages in the USA in 2017. Unfortunately, there were also about 827,000 divorces. Let's face it—far too many people get divorced. As we have said for the past 37 years, most marriages are worth saving, but it takes hard work to do so.

The focus of our research over the years has been on those who have made their marriages work. However, we are also constantly reminded that some marriages need help. Some marriages need a third-party to help them make their marriage survive and thrive.

Oftentimes, reaching out to a qualified marriage counselor can save a marriage. And while a good marriage counselor can be important to sustaining your relationship, a bad counselor can often cause even more harm.

As you seek someone to help your marriage work through the issues confronting it, **it is critical to find marriage advice from a counselor who exhibits these seven characteristics:**

1. Great marriage counselors never talk jargon with their clients when Simple Truths are required.

Here's the bottom line—it doesn't matter if your marital relationship is at "Stage 4." Moreover, does it really matter if your marriage, like most marriages, goes through so-called "stages of marriage?" How does that knowledge help your marriage?

The best help a counselor can give you is to lead you and your spouse through whatever challenges your marriage is facing without resorting to jargon that you don't understand. Working through the trying times in a marriage is not about the mystical powers of your counselor. Rather, it is about your relationship and their ability to help you and your spouse reach resolution about important issues that confront you.

2. Great marriage counselors don't over-intellectualize marriage and marital conflicts.

Without a doubt, love is something you feel—in your heart, your soul, and in your being. When your relationship needs help, the last thing you need is for someone to tell you that what you and your spouse are feeling with regard to your relationship can be explained by some entry in the Diagnostic and Statistical Manual of Mental Disorders (currently referred to as DSM-V), the most widely-used psychiatric/psychological reference book and standard diagnostic tool used by mental health professionals worldwide.

Don't get us wrong, the Manual is a great reference source, but in the end, an intellectual tool can't measure love! Love is an emotion, and the best counselors know this. They act as a "guide on the side" as you and the one you love address the challenges confronting your marriage.

The best marriage counselors help your marriage get in touch with the respective emotions of you and your spouse. They help you feel the emotions that cause you to come to grips with what you want from your marriage.

3. Great marriage counselors are NOT advocates for a particular marital perspective. Instead, they focus on YOUR marriage.

Here's a truism you can take to the bank—it is not the role of the marriage counselor to be an advocate for anything while counseling you and your spouse about your marital problems!

Frankly, their personal opinions are not relevant to your marriage. Their stories about their marriage, their parent's marriage, or other marriages they have treated do not matter when it comes to YOUR marriage. Your marriage is, in most ways, unique! The answers you and your spouse are seeking about your marriage are not always informed by the experiences of others.

While common positive themes run through the best marriages, and while there are telltale signs of failing marriages, in the end, each marriage that is in failure is in failure for reasons that are unique to that marriage.

4. Great marriage counselors don't make marriage too difficult to understand. They know that "simple things matter."

Our research on successful marriage has revealed that successful marriage is, in fact, simple to understand! The problem now and always has been this—marriages fail most often because couples do not do the simple things required to make their marriage work!

A marriage counselor failing to explain and focus on the simple things required to have a successful relationship, can make the marriage relationship seem more difficult than it really is. Unfortunately, when a counselor makes marriage too difficult to understand, they inhibit the relationship development of the couple they are trying to help.

The best marriage counselors work by guiding you and your spouse to understand that acts of kindness, respect, love, and caring must occur every day of the year consistently for your marriage relationship to be successful.

5. Great marriage counselors do NOT choose sides in a marital dispute during counseling.

If you are in marriage counseling, look for this action from you marriage counselor—if they take sides—if they choose the perspective of one of you over the other—get a different counselor!

Settling or resolving a marital dispute requires objectivity on the part of your counselor. The best marriage counselors understand that unconditional positive regard for their clients is of the utmost importance. Making judgments, taking sides, and advocating for one or the other can be destructive. Choosing sides can fracture the trust that is required in marital counseling.

6. Great marriage counselors understand the old axiom that most marriages are worth saving, but not all.

We have said for years that most marriages are worth saving, BUT NOT ALL! Most couples that go into marriage counseling truly believe that their marriage is worth saving and can be saved. In their heart of hearts, they want their marriage to be successful.

But truth is, some marriages are NOT worth saving. Some marriages have traveled so far down the path of no return that there is no hope. They are so beleaguered by physical and mental abuse that they cannot and should not be saved. The consequence of saving such a marriage can be destructive.

Marriage counselors make a mistake when they tell you that they can save every marriage with work. They must understand their limitations and the fact that sometimes saving an abusive relationship is downright dangerous.

7. *Great marriage counselors do not interject personal opinions and experiences into the counseling session.*

The research on marriage counseling over the decades is clear—the best marriage counselor's hold back expressing their personal opinions and experiences during the marriage counseling session.

Here is a telltale sign—you are having an exchange during your therapy session and your counselor says something like this, "Well, my wife and I have never experienced what you and your spouse are experiencing."

The question is, who cares! The relationship your marriage counselor has with his or her wife or others is irrelevant to your marital relationship. And frankly, the interjection by the counselor of his or her own personal marital relationship teeters on the edge of unethical behavior on their part.

When you are participating in marriage counseling you are in a very vulnerable position. You deserve the best counseling you and your spouse can get. Counselors are not selling snake oil. They are selling their expertise, their professional judgment, and their years of training as professional counselors. They do not have the right to be incompetent and make any of these mistakes. When you seek marriage counseling you have the right to seek it from a trained and competent professional who meets the requisite requirements to be a marriage counselor.

❦

HOW CAN MARRIAGE SURVIVE
THE CHALLENGES?

IN MARRIAGE SIMPLE THINGS MATTER

Debunking the Divorce Rate Myth

*But the truth is, the suggestion that
there is a 50% divorce rate in America
is simply wrong, wrong, wrong!*

*L*ET'S FACE IT, A LOT OF
couples contemplating marriage get discouraged by the oft-quoted
statistic that 50% of marriages in America end in divorce. Who
could blame them? Who wants to get into relationships where there
is the expectation of failure half the time! But the truth is, the
suggestion that there is a 50% divorce rate in American is simply
wrong, wrong, wrong! We would like to de-bunk that myth, that
fiction, that urban legend!

Where did such a notion come from? What could be the
motivation of groups and individuals that promulgate such a
falsehood? Do they want to discourage traditional marriage? Do
they have a political agenda? Have they simply offered a conclusion
based on their faulty analysis of the available data? Or worse yet,
have they intentionally misrepresented what we know about
marriage and divorce in America in order to undermine this great
social institution?

The answer we guess is probably all of the above to some extent.
Clearly, it is hard to get into the hearts and minds of human beings.
Without a doubt, it is difficult to determine the motivations of

others. So, we will resist talking about the motives of folks and simply deal with the facts about divorce in America. And here are the facts.

First of all, the divorce rate is not nearly as high as it is often reported in the popular media. We need to change that perception because it can be a discouraging message to those contemplating marriage.

The divorce rate in America is not 50% for first-time marriages, period! For example, most experts we have talked to believe the rate is closer to 40%. We ourselves have estimated the rate in previous writings at somewhere between 35% and 40%. A 2001 survey by researcher George Barna estimated that 34% of American's who have ever been married have ever been divorced. Several studies we have reviewed actually estimated the divorce rate to be less than 20%. It is our considered opinion that the 20% and less figures are too low, but one thing is clear—more than 60% of marriages are successful!

Pinning down the exact divorce rate in America is certainly complicated. Many studies have been done, many numbers crunched, and many conclusions drawn. But the truth of the matters is, the national per capita divorce rate has declined steadily since its peak in 1981 and *is now at the lowest level since 1970.* The fact that the per capita divorce has declined should be cause for celebration.

Secondly, there are a number of factors that can reduce the divorce rate and rather than dwelling on the perceived chances of failure of a marriage we should be looking for reasons why most marriages do not fail—do not end in divorce.

Over the years we have seen a positive trend developing and it is highly encouraging to us. It is clear to us that more and more couples are working harder and harder to make their marriage work. They are investing solid efforts at strengthening their marriage. They read books like ours on the subject—*Building A Love That Lasts,* they participate in marriage enrichment programs, they seek counseling from a qualified professional counselor or psychologist, and they learn to do the simple things that make marriage work each and every day of their lives together.

The good news—more and more couples are committed to making their marriage work! In a society that is often characterized as "a disposable society," marriage should not be one of those things we routinely dispose of! As we have said many times before, not all marriages are worth saving, *but most are and can be saved!*

And thirdly, we need to debunk the many myths about how to ensure a successful relationship. And here's one to begin with. Despite the belief of many, living together while not married does not necessarily promote a happy and successful relationship. For example, the Centers for Disease Control reported that there is only a 20% chance that first marriages will end in divorce in the first five years. On the other hand, the separation rate in the first five years for those cohabiting is a *whopping 49%!* These data seem to fly in the face of those who suggest that giving marriage a trial run or just cohabiting instead of marrying at all, is the way to go. It seems these advice givers need to check their facts about what works.

There is a corollary to the aforementioned notion about living together. Some researchers have reported that the highest risk factor for divorce is moving in together prior to marriage! Couples who do this have *a far greater risk of divorce.* In fact, couples who cohabitat before marriage—who give their "marriage" a trial run— have a divorce rate more than twice as high. Some studies suggest it is as high as 85%. Talk about the destruction of a myth!

We know that second and third marriages have high failure rates. Most studies report that second marriages have about a two out of three chance of failure—third marriages about a 75%

chance. These second and third marriages (as well as those married four or more times) get lumped into divorce equations that are often reported. The simple truth is, the "impact rate" of divorce—those individuals that divorce actually impacts—is clearly much lower than the oft-reported rate of 50%. Those married for the first time just need to learn to get it right the first time!

So what are the factors that have major implications for the risk of divorce? Barbara Whitehead and David Popenoe in their book entitled *The State of Our Unions* (2004) reported the following:

1. **Couples with annal incomes over $50,000 (vs. under $25,000) have a reduced risk of divorce of 30%.** The message here is that couples contemplating marriage would be well advised to have income-producing jobs with stability before they get married.

2. *Couples who have a baby seven months or more after marriage (vs. before marriage) have a reduced risk of divorce of 24%.* The message here should be clear – bring children into the world when your marriage is ready.

3. *Couples who are 25 years of age (vs. under 18) have a 24% less risk of divorce.* The American divorce rate has been going down since 1981 because people in love are waiting longer to get married. Gaining education, experience, and the wisdom that comes with age will certainly contribute to the success of a marriage.

4. *Couples that consider themselves religious or spiritual (vs. not) are 14% less likely to get divorced.* Faith and spirituality contribute to the sense of *oneness* felt by successfully married couples.

5. *Couples who have some college (vs. high-school dropout) have a 13% less chance of divorce.* Education almost always leads to enlightenment and understanding, and more tolerance for the

views of others. All are so critically important in successful marriages.

In summary, reasonably well-educated couples with a decent income, who are religious or spiritual, who wait awhile to have children, who come from intact families, and who marry later in life (25 and beyond), have a greatly reduced chance of divorce.

The American divorce rate is much lower than often reported. And considering that the average American has a 80%+ chance of being married at least once in their lifetime, it is nice to know that there is much we can do as individuals and as couples in love to make marriage work—to make marriage successful.

Stressed Out?
Nine Strategies for Coping

Stress can bring a whole new set of challenges to your marriage.

A RECENT STUDY found that a stressful relationship can damage your health and even kill you! Stress in a marriage can in fact, take a very serious toll on your relationship with your spouse. In fact, the impact that a stressful relationship can have on your health and that of your spouse can actually kill you!

According to a recent Danish study, arguing and worrying over family problems may lead to an increased risk of dying in middle age. "Stressful social relations in private life are associated with a two to three-times increased risk of dying," said lead researcher Dr. Rikke Lund, an associate professor in the department of public health at the University of Copenhagen.

What are the warning signs that your relationship is suffering? What can you do to keep your love alive while dealing with stress? How can you protect your health and the health of your spouse by dealing with marital stress effectively?

Make no mistake about it, the negative impact of stress on your marriage and our personal health can be substantial! Stress can bring a whole new set of challenges to your marriage. But the truth is, the damage can be prevented.

Our research over the years suggests that there are a number of useful strategies that you can use to not only deal with the everyday stresses of marriage, but that can also strengthen your marriage at the same time and, perhaps, save your life.

Nine strategies for dealing with stress in your marriage:

1. *Talk openly about your feelings and emotions as they relate to stress in your marriage.* In times of stress the tendency is to keep everything bottled up inside or explode at the slightest disagreement. However, this approach will not work if you want your marriage to survive and thrive. In successful marriages couples talk about everything.

* Share with your spouse insights about everything—the good, the bad and the ugly.

* Make a conscious effort to hear what your spouse is really saying with an attitude of acceptance.

* Become each other's best friend with unconditional support, total trust and complete honesty.

2. *Approach all financial challenges with teamwork and open communication.* Balancing the family budget requires teamwork, especially when introducing children into your marriage, dealing with unusual financial burdens, or losing a job comes your way. People in love support each other through thick and thin—through tough times and uncertainty. If you don't work together to address head-on the economic challenges and stresses on your marriage, there is little hope of success.

* Keep the lines of communication open regarding your financial situation.

* Work together to determine your common financial goals.

* Never make a major purchase without talking it over with your spouse and sleeping on it.

3. *Don't blame each other when things get tough, as casting blame never solved a problem.* The blame game doesn't work in love and marriage and it is destructive. There is a natural tendency in tough times to blame the one you love for your collective misfortune and stress, but people in love don't blame, castigate, or chastise each other in challenging times.

* No matter how you feel, always treat your spouse with respect and love.

* The truth is, there usually is no one person to blame. Figure out how you contributed to the problem and what you can do differently in the future.

* Give your spouse's opinion serious consideration as you work together to discover solutions to your problems.

4. *Don't wallow in self-pity.* No problem has ever been solved by feeling sorry for yourself or your situation. It is a wasted emotion. Successful couples grab "the bull by the horns" and work for solutions—recognizing that running a household is not easy. Making a family work is, clearly, difficult even in the best of times and even more challenging when you have many stressors to deal with.

* Sit down with your spouse to figure out possible solutions to your problem and determine a plan that both of you can support.

* Celebrate your successes as you accomplish each step of the plan. Feeling like you are moving in a positive direction helps eliminate self-pity.

5. *Make a concerted effort to keep the flame of your love affair alive with each other everyday.* What type of priority do you place on making time for fun and romance with each other in your hectic lives? Can you rattle off a list of activities, topics and places you and your spouse include in your personal book of fun and romance?

* Make a point of touching your spouse in a loving way at least ten times a day.

* Carve out time to have a romantic date with each other, bring home flowers, get a hotel room, go for a long walk together, drink a bottle of wine watching the sunset, write a love note, and snuggle in bed a little longer in the morning.

* Sit and face your spouse using Braille to discover all of their intricate features.

6. *Enhance your love relationship by providing each other occasional time for privacy and aloneness.* The recognition of the absolute need for privacy and aloneness is, in our judgment after analyzing thousands of interviews, critical to successful marriages. We live such hectic lives at work and at home that the time to be alone with our own thoughts is paramount to our ability to engage in any meaningful communication with each other. The quality of communication can only be enhanced between the two of you after refreshing your mind and spirit with alone time. You have to belong to yourself before you can belong to others.

* The amount of time available to satisfy these two needs varies from one marriage to another and from one marriage partner to another, and can increase during times of stress. Talk with your spouse about each of your needs and desires for privacy and alone time.

* Work together to determine a plan that you both will honor to allow each other occasional time for privacy and aloneness.

7. **Remember that "In Marriage Simple Things Matter" and they need to be practiced daily.** Thirty-seven years of research on love and successful marriage has taught us many things, but first and foremost—no love has blossomed or been sustained without doing the simple things. Big things don't matter until your relationship has mastered the art of doing the simple things day in and day out in your relationship with the one you love. Too often when we are engaged in stressful life situations we forget to just do the simple things for the one we love the most. The point is, simple things matter and when you practice doing them, they accumulate.

* Make a list of 20 simple things you will do to make your spouse's life better. Examples: Remember to say thank you, call when you are going to be late, leave a sticky love note on your lover's wallet or purse.

* Be more generous with your time for each other.

* Engage in simple acts of kindness and spontaneous feel good moments.

8. **Develop a network of support from family, friends, and relatives.** You and your spouse do not have to deal with the stress all by yourself. Don't be deluded into thinking you can or even should do it alone. Your friends and family want to support you through thick and thin. Take full advantage of their willingness to help.

* Cultivate good relationships with your family, friends and relatives. They can be your best supporters in times of need.

* Don't be shy about asking for help from your family, aunts, uncles or neighbors.

9. Staying healthy and happy, both physically and mentally, should be the highest priority of both you and your spouse. It is nearly impossible to take care of others when you don't take of yourself.

* Live healthier—take your vitamins and medications, eat lots of fruits and vegetables, cut down the use of alcohol and nicotine.

* Engage in a daily exercise program with your spouse.

* Don't forget your annual physical exams.

Dealing with the many stressors in your marriage and in life can be a real challenge. Dealing with them effectively could not only save your marriage, but save your life.

Six Fatal Mistakes that
Can Destroy Your Marriage

*Believing in happily ever after
can lead to six deadly mistakes!*

ANY NEWLYWEDS wonder what ever happened to "happily ever after." As soon as problems associated with living together as a married couple begin to arise, the fantasy concept of marriage is shattered for many. They have created unrealistic expectations for their lives together, so they are not prepared for the inevitable bumps in the road that occur. They struggle when trying to resolve even the most basic issues such as: Who prepares dinner? How to pay for the needed car repairs? Who takes out the garbage? How to find time for your own interests? How to deal with too little money to live the lifestyle you thought you would have?

From our research throughout the world, we have discovered the six most common mistakes married couples make during the early years of their marriage. Avoiding these six deadly mistakes can help you and your spouse form the foundation of a long lasting, happy and successful marriage.

Six ways to avoid making the deadly mistakes that can destroy a promising marriage:

1. Never go to bed mad at each other. *This is the number one piece of advice given to us from successfully married couples around the world.* Don't listen to the "so called experts" who say you can sleep on it and talk about it in the morning when you are calmer. This is just NOT true. Going to bed angry is toxic!

2. Don't keep score. Keeping track of wins and losses leads to unhealthy competition and holding grudges. Couples should never ignore bothersome behaviors, but there can be no winners and losers in a great marriage. You can't hold grudges and you shouldn't cast blame when things go wrong. Don't be afraid to argue and debate an issue. Just remember to fight fair and learn to argue effectively. It is the only way to have a lasting partnership.

3. Never lie to your spouse. Little white lies and broken promises erode the glue that holds a marriage together. Even small lies can form a habit of dishonesty in your relationship. Dishonesty erodes the very essence of the bond between the two of you. Never promise what you cannot deliver. Trust is the foundation of any lasting relationship.

4. Never make assumptions. Assumptions lead to trouble. You should ask your spouse what he or she likes, dislikes, enjoys, thinks or feels. The old adage is certainly true that to assume is to make an "ass out of you and me!" And the corollary is, never ignore behaviors in your spouse that bother you. Your relationship will be strengthened if you talk out issues calmly and respectfully instead of assuming things will get better.

5. Don't run up a mountain of debt when you first get married. Racking up too much debt is pure poison when it comes to your marriage. Keep the use of credit cards under control. The single greatest cause of divorce and marital discourse is debt and other financial-related issues.

6. *Deal with the stress in your relationship.* Stress is something most people don't think about. It just comes on suddenly and you don't know why you feel the way you do. Taking a breathe when you are feeling overwhelmed with stress helps you put things in perspective. Figuring out the what, when, where, why and how stress is impacting you and your relationship is a critical step in letting go of those negative feelings. You cannot build a solid lifelong relationship until you know how to deal with stress from outside sources, stress from within the relationship or stress from worrying about things that may never happen.

Even the most happily married couples tell us that marriage is not fair, just, and beautiful all the time. Just like life, marriage comes with its ups and downs. If you go into marriage believing it will be like a Hollywood movie with roses, sunshine, no responsibilities, and no setbacks, you are in for a big disappointment. Every successful marriage has to deal with setbacks.

Creating a successful marriage is not always the easiest thing to do. But if you work to avoid making the six deadly mistakes most often made by newlyweds, you will be well on your way to creating your own real "happily ever after" story together. You will discover what we and other happily married couples have discovered over the decades—a successful marriage is an accumulation of having done the simple things. A great marriage is no more complicated than that!

Here is the truth of the matter—having a great marriage takes lots of hard work. A long-lasting and happy marriage doesn't occur by accident, it requires the investment of productive effort in making it successful. Don't make those fatal mistakes. Your marriage may not survive them.

❦

How to Talk Serious
with Your Mate

Happily married couples attribute their marital
success first and foremost to the fact that they
have honed their communication skills over time.

OVER THE MANY YEARS
we have been conducting research about love and marriage, we are
continually reminded of the important role effective communication between couples plays in the overall health and well being of
their relationship.

The "heart of the matter" is this—successfully married couples
report a high level of satisfaction with the way they communicate
with each other, and they attribute their marital success first and
foremost to the fact that they have honed their communication
skills over time. Oh sure, in the early years even successfully
married couples report that they struggled with all this, but over
time they got better and better at it because they kept working at it.

So, what are the lessons we have learned from those couples that
communicate effectively on just about every level. As we poured
over our many interview notes, important themes began to emerge
and we are pleased to share them with you.

1. ***Effective marital communication always begins with proper***
engagement and in a proper context. There is a time and

place for everything and communicating effectively with each other is no exception. Talking about serious matters cannot occur effectively when dealing with chaos—children who need to be fed, a blaring television in the background, when both of you have iPhones plugged into your ears, or when you are in different rooms of the house engaging in different activities, where shouting is the only alternative!

2. *There is proper etiquette to follow in effective communication.* Remember, you can't communicate effectively with each other when you are both talking at the same time. It's hard to listen when one or the other is doing all of the talking! You can't hear effectively if you both are shouting at each other. It is always better to lower your voices and speak in a calm manner. Remember, it is never a good idea to blame, accuse, call names, or make nasty remarks. Being ready to communicate and follow these basic rules of engagement will get you off to a good start.

3. *Discussions about serious issues must always begin with agreement about what the issues really are.* Until you work to identify the issue, establish the parameters of the discussion, and agree to solve the problem or issue together, it is hard, if not impossible, to get your communication with each other up to the level required for proper resolution of the challenge you are confronting. Sometimes the debates and discussions with each other become like two ships passing in the night – they never see, listen, or learn from each other— they are just two ships passing in the night.

4. *A fruitful conversation about important matters always begins with the brainstorming of ideas.* It is important to get your respective ideas out on the table. Talk about the relative strengths and weaknesses of each. Agree on ideas worth exploring. When you agree on a plan, stick to it. When the

two of you share the responsibility for the direction or directions you take, you will both feel much more buy-in and commitment, and you will be much more willing to share responsibility for the outcome, good or bad.

5. ***The precursor to successful marital communication is confidence.*** Developing the ability to communicate effectively allows for an open and honest expression of opinions and ideas. Being allowed to express a contrary opinion without shouting it out is one of the first signs that you are becoming a confident communicator with your mate. Having you or your spouse disagree with each other's opinions without either getting defensive or unnecessarily argumentative is a clear sign of maturity in your communicative relationship. Successfully married couples tell us they learned these lessons early on and worked on being confident in their expressions everyday. It may start slow early in your relationship but daily practice builds momentum. When either or both mates lack confidence in their ability to communicate with their spouse, effective communication is greatly hindered.

6. ***Never, we repeat, never be judgmental when debating issues with your mate.*** Passing judgment on an idea at the drop of a hat is usually the death of open and honest debate between two people. When you say something like, "That is a stupid idea" or "That is about the dumbest thing I have ever heard," you are putting an arrow through your spouse, and it hurts! When they close down and refuse to further discuss the issue(s) you were debating, then all exchanges end. No solutions are found. And the truth is, the wounds caused by this action further erode the ability of the two of you to engage in healthy exchanges—in healthy debate in the future.

7. ***Simple things matter when it comes to discussions about tough or challenging issues.*** When serious issues arise and

the two of you need to deal with them, there are some simple things that you can do to insure that your exchanges become part of a rational discussion rather than an argument or an endless diatribe about why your mate is wrong. Learn these simple lessons—listen intently to what your spouse is saying; make eye contact with them; turn off all electronic appliances (TV, radio, music, iPhone, etc.) so as not to be distracted during your conversation; seek clarification when you don't understand or comprehend something; hold hands when you debate; and never make disagreements personal. Lessons to live by, for sure!

The successfully married couples we have interviewed over the years report to us that they never felt invalidated by their spouse, they always felt their arguments were heard, and their opinions always mattered.

Having a successful marriage is not all that complicated. Learn the simple lessons of communication that these wonderful couples have taught us—and have now taught you!

How to Fight Fair

*Fighting and arguing are just as much
a part of marriage as having sex*

LEARNING HOW TO FIGHT
fair and to make appropriate compromises will go a long way to
keeping your relationship strong. Compromise is rarely 50/50.
Some days it is 90/10; some days it is 60/40; and some days it really
is 50/50. Compromise is what marriage is all about. Whether it is
what to make for dinner, what movie to see, when to have children,
where to live or what color to paint the living room, the two of you
have to make the decisions together that both of you can support
after the decision is made.

Fighting and arguing are just as much a part of marriage as
having sex. While it is a fact that fighting is a natural part of relating
to another human being, there are rules you can follow to find ways
to come to solutions without destroying the fabric of your relationship.

Here are the seven rules of engagement for fighting fair:

1. ***Fight in a calm manner.*** Don't shout or throw things or rant
   about the situation. Think about what you are going to say
   before it actually comes flowing out of your mouth. Keep
   your body language in tact. In other words, don't take a

position of anger or hostility before one word is even spoken. Relax as much as you can and try to put down the anger you are feeling to keep a calm demeanor.

2. ***No name calling or ugly verbiage about your spouse.*** Don't let the argument degrade into a battle of personal insults. It doesn't address the issues and can do lasting damage to your relationship with each other even if you didn't mean what you said. You can't take back your words!

3. ***You are an adult, act like it.*** Don't have a temper tantrum! Don't just sit there looking mad without saying anything. Engage in the conversation with the thought of how can we solve this problem together as adults.

4. ***Keep the argument logical and focused on the issues at hand.*** Don't wander off topic to old battles or old scars. Determine what the problem is, what issues need to be dealt with and what are the possible solutions. If you focus on determining which solution would work best, it keeps you moving toward an end result, rather than diverting your attention to negative side issues.

5. ***Don't cast blame.*** It doesn't matter who is right or wrong. It doesn't matter whose fault it is. You share the problems together and you have to share the solutions together. What you discover is that when you figure out how to solve the problem and you get on with the solution working as a team, the two of you can tackle anything that comes your way.

6. ***Don't hold grudges.*** As soon as the issue has been resolved, forget it and move on. The worst thing you can do is remind your spouse of the fight or problems. That means no gloating if you were right and no reminding him or her constantly about how mad you still are. Couples with great marriages tell us that they have a short memory when it comes time to

their past arguments. In fact, when asked, they can't even remember what they were arguing about or who did what. That is the way it should be.

7. *As we have said many times before, NEVER go to bed mad at each other.* Settle your fight before you go to bed, no matter how long it takes. You can defer the ultimate decision on an issue until further discussion the next day, but you can't go to bed mad at each other.

Remember, it is perfectly okay to argue and debate with your spouse. Better solutions are often arrived at when you engage in wholesome debate. Learning how to argue effectively is critically important to a healthy marriage and to a healthy relationship.

Five Tips to Jerk Your Marriage from Negative to Positive

An abrupt injection of positivity

into your marriage

can have surprising effects.

*W*ITH OUR FAST PACED society and the extreme demands hitting us from every side, more and more couples find negativity taking over their marriage. An abrupt injection of positivity into your relationship is the only way to change the environment before it is too late.

From our research over many years, we have discovered tips they use to keep their relationships positive. **Here are the 5 tips you can use to jerk your marriage from to positive:**

1. *Take an honest look at what YOU could do differently to improve your relationship.* Could you spend more time with your spouse, or take more interest in their hobbies, or stop pointing out their weaknesses or talk more openly about what is bothering you?

2. *When dealing with a marital crisis avoid saying:*

   * It's your fault! Sometimes, a financial decision goes bad or your child gets in trouble at school. Blame doesn't work!

* I told you so! These four words are rarely ever used in successful marriages.

* Saying , "I am upset with you about . . ." in a public setting.

* "Why do you always . . ." Focusing on your spouse's weakness rather than building on their strengths will only increase their weakness and diminish their strength.

* Ask for your spouse's opinion and then do the opposite.

3. ***Repair your spirit and your balance.*** Take the steps to get healthy mentally and physically. You can't turn off the negativity when you are in an unhealthy state. You need to heal yourself first.

4. ***Successful couples build positive interactions with each other on a daily basis.*** Begin your interactions with positive comments. Comment on something your spouse has done that was good, helpful or kind. Notice the small things and make a nice comment about them. If your spouse begins a conversation with a negative comment or is upset, don't jump down their throat with a negative response. Bite your tongue and wait to comment until you can turn your thoughts into a positive comment. It is amazing how often an entire conversation can be changed with a positive comment.

5. ***Appreciate what you have! If you have good health, a place to live, or a job, you already have more than most people in the world.*** Focus on the positives. Talk openly about them. Your happiness will begin putting the spark back in the relationship.

Remember, getting out of a negative spiral begins with one positive action, then another, until a habit of positive actions is built in to your relationship.

Are Your Finances
Driving You Crazy?
Seven Sanity Saving Strategies

Money—or the lack of it—

is the number one cause of

arguments in a marriage.

WHEN FINANCIAL problems become the main source of stress in your marriage, it is time to act. Just hoping your money problems will go away will not solve them. Money—or the lack of it—is the number one cause of arguments in a marriage. It takes a real commitment from both of you working as a team with common financial goals to stay ahead of money problems.

People in love support each other through thick and thin—through good and bad financial times. People in love don't blame, castigate, or chastise each other when making financial decisions. They work together to make ends meet and to prepare for tomorrow.

If you address head-on the economic challenges in your marriage, your chances of success get a whole lot better. The thousands of happily married couples we have interviewed talk about working together to maintain their financial stability. Interestingly, many of these successfully married couples were open about their financial difficulties and the strategies they employ to keep their financial house in order.

Here are the seven most critical actions you need to take to keep your money problems from destroying your marriage:

1. *Get on the same page with your spouse.* You are in this together, so make it a team effort. These are after all our problems not my problems and your problems. Don't wallow in self-pity. It is a wasted emotion. No problem has ever been solved by feeling sorry for yourself or your situation. Work together to make ends meet and to prepare for tomorrow.

2. *Communicate, communicate, communicate!* Open and regular communication about all financial goals, choices and commitments is the only way to form a plan that will work. In a marriage you must share both the joys of financial success and the burdens of financial setbacks. Never argue and get angry at each other over finances. Casting blame and calling your spouse names will not solve your financial problems! If you keep in touch regarding your financial situation you are much more likely to avoid commitments that place a strain or burden on your relationship. The old adage—an ounce of prevention is worth a pound of cure—is truly applicable regarding marital finances.

3. *Develop a realistic budget—one that both of you can live with.* The number one cause of stress in marital relationships is money problems often caused by running up a "butt load" of debt. Too much month at the end of each paycheck makes it tough to relax and enjoy life together. Work out a budget together and stick to it. Develop a realistic budget and set common financial goals. Take out a sheet of paper and write down all of your regular monthly expenses including housing, food, cars, etc. Then in the next column write down your monthly income. See what is left after the fixed expenses

(i.e. food, housing, etc.). Then decide what kind of limits you both will put on spending money and what kind of priorities you both feel are important to maintain. If your expenses are greater than your income, immediately discuss what expenses can be eliminated or how you can add income. Put off purchasing anything that you can until you save enough money to pay for it. Don't take too long in resolving this dilemma, since the kind of stress this puts on a marriage can be extremely damaging.

4. ***Mutually agree on your routine spending habits.*** Taking the time to analyze what each of you routinely spend money on can be just as important as making decisions about major spending issues. If one of you is regularly purchasing new clothes, hobby supplies, recreational items, etc. while the other one is skimping on everything to make ends meet, open discussion and changes need to occur immediately. Many times we have observed routine spending habits to be problematic and often overlooked because each purchase doesn't seem like it amounts to very much money by itself. However, if it is a regular pattern of spending, the amounts can add up quickly to become major financial problems.

5. ***Never make a major purchase without talking it over with your spouse and sleeping on it.*** You would be surprised at the number of purchases you don't make if you sleep on it! Couple communication on this matter will insure to a large extent that you both agree on the purchase, thus preventing a serious faultfinding session later if the decision was a bad one from a financial point of view. This notion also promotes sharing. What you own in a marriage should be yours together . . . not yours and mine. We are often asked, "What is a major purchase?" Excellent question! Major varies from one couple to another. Obviously, a house, an automobile, or a large appliance qualifies as major to most couples. After

that, the definition runs the full gamut. There have been times in our marriage when making a $10.00 purchase was a monumental decision, and other times when we felt that a $200.00 purchase was major. The notion of "major" varies from couple to couple and depends to a large extent on your financial situation. You will have to decide . . . but you must decide together!

6. ***Taking ACTION together is the best way of solving your financial problems.*** Agree on a course of action to live within your means and pay off your debts. Using the budget you developed together provides the clarity of purpose necessary for finding a solution to any financial problems that occur. Pay all of your bills together. That doesn't mean both of you have to actually sit down together to pay the bills. Rather, it means that both of you know exactly what the bills are and what is being paid. Climbing out of financial difficulties takes focus, a positive team approach, and ACTION.

7. ***Celebrate each time you have a financial success such as paying off a credit card or finding a way to cut expenses.*** Fiscal responsibility is a virtue. Taking time to celebrate together creates the feeling that the next goal is even more achievable.

If all else fails and you are in over your heads financially, seek professional financial counseling. Don't show so much pride that you can't or won't seek help. Your marriage is worth saving from financial disaster. Talk to your banker—they want you to succeed financially, it is in their best interest—or a financial planner, or an accountant, or get a referral from a friend. Most financial problems are solvable! Don't bury your heads in the sand and pretend that the problems will disappear. There is one thing that always seems to be true . . . financial problems do not go away; they only get worse if you don't take steps to solve them. Don't allow finances to unravel the beautiful relationship you have with your spouse. Make sense of your dollars . . . start today!

While finances are the number one cause of marital disagreements, once you solve your financial issues you can focus again on what really matters—being in love with someone you trust with your love, your sacred honor, and with your life.

Don't Let a Messy World
Destroy Your Marriage

How we deal with the stressors
of the world, are feelings
and emotions we can control.

O KAY, LET'S FACE IT,
the world today is in many ways a mess. The daily doses of bad news
you watch on your television; the steady drumbeat of bad news in
your newspaper; the bombardment of negativity on the Internet,
television, and on the radio; and the constant negative exchanges
you have with others on social media—much of it from your "so-
called friends" (putting you down, criticizing you, making fun of
you, putting you on the defensive, embarrassing you in front of
others, etc.); *is enough to make you want to crawl in a hole and hide!*

But there is a better solution if you want to save your relationships with others, especially your husband/wife or "significant
other."

You see, getting in the doldrums—letting your psychic be
impacted in negative ways by the constant negativity in the news
and in social media—can begin to bring you down and affect you
and your relationships with others in terrible and unproductive
ways.

And remember this—if you spend too much of your day being told how awful everything is, it WILL affect the way you feel, the way you relate to others—especially the ones you love—and the way you love. Make no mistake about it!

So, how do you prevent and/or combat the daily bombardment of the negative things you experience? How do you keep negativity from affecting your relationships with those you love, especially your spouse? How do you "keep yourself together" in a psychological sense? We have discovered four effective solutions based on our research with successful marriage on all seven continents of the world. **Here are the four effective solutions in a nutshell:**

1. *You need to set up a plan of action immediately* that limits on a daily basis the amount of news you watch, what you read in the newspaper, and what you consume from the Internet. Reading all the negative stuff will eventually impact the way you view the world, yourself, and those you interact with on a daily basis. Listening to and reading the constant bombardment of negative news is, in many ways, like being in a prisoner-of-war camp—you begin to believe and feel all that which you read—and in the end, it consumes you—it impacts your very being! You think the world is falling apart! Be informed, but enough is enough! Being informed of local, national, and world events does not require you to be a slave to negative news. Limit your news intake.

2. *Exercise is a great physical and psychological stress reliever! Exercise often.* The truth of the matter is this—exercise is not only good for you physically, it is good for you psychologically and emotionally. Exercise is, as a fitness enthusiast friend of ours recently said, "The elixir for the soul." Exercise releases chemicals in your body that puts you in a "good place." Exercise makes you feel good about yourself—it puts you in a "happy place" and releases the stressors that limit you and

your relationships on a daily basis. Some kinesiologists believe that these secret chemicals are "Endorphins," which act as a kind of sedative that reduces "pain"—psychologically and physically. Exercise often! Your mind and body will appreciate it more than you know.

3. ***Everyday of your life do something positive for somebody!*** Engage in acts of kindness. Say something nice to a friend or a stranger. Become a great purveyor of love! There is one simple rule of the Universe—a smile requires fewer muscles to carry out than a frown. Be a positive person. Tell the ones you love and the strangers you meet something positive. You will be astonished at how much better the world will seem AND become! When somebody throws a negative at you, respond with something positive. It will blow their mind, trust us on this one. It is so easy to be a positive person and by being so, you will relieve much of your stress and the stress of the one you said something nice to!

4. ***Each day of your life, observe and embrace the beauty around you.*** The world is a beautiful place for the most part. Look for the beauty in it each day of your life. Smell the flowers, watch the sunsets, get up for a sunrise, hold hands with the one you love while you share a glass of wine on the back porch or deck, and make note of the incredible beauty that surrounds you everyday. There is a simple truth here— the world is a beautiful place and when you notice its wonderful beauty, you won't have time to wallow in self-pity, be angry, experience frustration, or be unhappy. We are not suggesting you not "feel" the pain of the world, your neighbors, and the like, but we are saying to you—put it all in proper perspective. This action will serve you well.

In the end, how we feel about ourselves, how we deal with those we love, and how we deal with the stressors of the world, are feelings and emotions we can control. Being informed, caring about others, being empathic with the plight of those less fortunate than us, and the like, does not require us to be constantly unhappy, sad, and depressed. These latter feelings only estrange us from those we love. Care, but don't be consumed by the bad news of the day. You have your life to live—you have others to love—you have a partner to love and cherish on a daily basis. You owe them and you this commitment.

Character in Love and Marriage

Character in a successful marriage
or relationship does matter,
and character is about trust.

*I*N CASE YOU DIDN'T KNOW it, there is a character element in love and loving relationships. People who say they love each other and then cheat on their spouse or lover, or lie to them on a regular basis, aren't really in love. Oh, many think they are, but they really are not. People who love each other have character when it comes to their marriage or relationship.

In our interviews with couples that have successful marriages we are always struck by their undying trust in each other. They literally trust each other with their lives, their fortune, and their sacred honor. The words they use to describe the one they love more often than not include words and expressions like trust, honesty, loyalty, respects me, admires me, always there for me, never lets me down, truthful, and never lies to me. Their trust for each other is about as complete as you can get. And when we ask couples in love during our interviews to place, in an overall sense, where their relationship is on a 10-point scale with 10 being "Absolute Trust," without exception, they say "10!" Isn't that wonderful? Remarkable? These are the couples that will celebrate their golden anniversaries together!

Trust is not something all loving relationships start with. For some couples the trust becomes complete in a few years. For others, it takes awhile. But one thing is for sure; happy and successful marriages and relationships survive and thrive on the basis of this trust. Trust is so pervasive in their relationship that they never give it a second thought. They expect it. It's always there. It is part of the fabric of their marriage.

There is one thing you can take to the bank—all people in love have faced temptations in their relationship. The pretty girl in the restaurant captures your fancy. The handsome man walking down the street draws your attention. The flirt at work is tempting at times. And, we will dare say, sometimes in every relationship you think about slipping in the sack with some of the beautiful people you meet. But here's where it stops—these are only fleeting moments of passing fancy. These are the moments of momentary lust for another human being that are not acted on. Why? People in love who are happy in their relationships control their urges because they know that while a moment of sexual fantasy is healthy and normal, following through and enjoying sexual satisfaction with someone other than their mate—cheating on their mate—is destructive to the loving and trusting relationship between them. It's okay to have sexual urges and fantasies regarding another person, but to act on them ruins all that trust. It destroys the ties that bind.

Couples who are truly in love in their relationship know that a few moments of sexual satisfaction can NEVER replace the loving, trusting, and caring relationship they have developed with their mate. As someone once said to us, "I have a marriage license but I didn't give up my looking license!" Admiring others in intimate ways is normal and healthy. But acting on those urges has ruined many a marriage and many a loving relationship.

Those wonderful couples we have interviewed resist these normal urges and temptations of life because they know their relationship is so much more important to them. Destroying the trust between them causes the foundation of their marriage to crumble.

Character in a successful marriage or relationship does matter, and character is about trust. Being honest and trustworthy is at the heart of all the best loving relationships we have studied. It really is a 10 on a 10-point scale. In our estimation, character is the foundation of true love! This is one of the most important lessons we have learned.

The Trials and Tribulations
of Having Children
in a Marriage

*You thought your marriage
was nearly perfect –
And Then…Along Came Kids.*

KIDS! WE LOVE THEM.
We cherish them.
They bring joy to our lives. When we have children in a marriage,
we understand finally, and once and for all, what eternity means.
While we are not immortal, we learn the meaning of everlasting life
when we are blessed with children. They make us feel like we will
live through time. We carry on through them. We know that
through them our lives will have meaning beyond our time on this
earth.

But our children are also a pain in the butt! They challenge us.
They taunt us. They demand much from us. They argue with us.
They divide us. They unite us. They run up one heck of a child-
care bill!

On the other hand, most successful marriages with children
wouldn't want it any other way. They know that without a doubt,
their children enrich their lives in innumerable ways. They value

their children immensely. But be clear regarding this—successfully married couples with children understand the challenges they pose to a blissful and romantic marital relationship.

You thought your marriage was nearly perfect—*And Then....Along Came Kids.* To quote Nora Ephron in *Heartburn:* "Having a first child is like throwing a hand grenade into a marriage." When you are responsible for the care of your children, you will, without a doubt, take on some enormous stresses.

After years and years of research around the world interviewing successfully married couples, one of our principal conclusions is— *the quality of the relationship between husband and wife trumps everything else in a marriage!* Get it right and good things follow. Get it wrong and lots of bad things often happen!

And you know why? Without a positive, loving, and thriving relationship between mom and dad, children often don't prosper, they are not well-adjusted, they don't do well in school, and they are not as healthy, both physically and mentally.

Our research over the years suggests that there are a number of useful tips that you can use to not only deal with the enormous stress of caregiving, but also strengthen your marriage at the same time. These tips appear on the surface to be simple, but in love, marriage and raising children the "Simple Things Matter".

Tips to Strengthen Your Marriage:

   1 Share openly with each other about feelings, emotions and stresses as they relate to caring for your children. In times of stress the tendency is to keep everything bottled up inside or explode at the slightest disagreement. However, this approach will not work if you want your marriage to survive and thrive. In successful marriages there are No Sacred Cows. Simply speaking, happily married couples talk about everything. All subjects are fair game. They trust each other. They rely on each other's good judgment. They depend upon each other for truth and straight talk. They share insights about everything—the good, the bad and the ugly. They are each other's best friends.

2. *Make a conscious effort to keep the flame of your love affair alive each and evey day.* Can you rattle off a list of activities, topics and places you and your spouse include in your personal book of fun and romance? Have you found what clears your mind and gives you an unobstructed view of your world together? What type of priority do you place on making time for fun and romance with each other in your hectic lives? If you cannot answer these questions easily, you need to start today by carving out time to have a romantic date with each other, bring home flowers, get a hotel room, go for a long walk together, drink a bottle of wine watching the sunset, write a love note, and snuggle in bed a little longer in the morning.

3. *Don't blame each other when things get tough, as casting blame never solved a problem.* The blame game doesn't work in love and marriage. It is destructive. There is a natural tendency in tough times to blame the one you love for your collective misfortune, but people in love don't blame, castigate, or chastise each other in challenging times. The truth is, there usually is no one to blame for the situation. Someone has to take care of the children and the job just fell to you.

4. *Don't wallow in self-pity; it is a wasted emotion.* No problem has ever been solved by feeling sorry for yourself or your situation. Trying to pretend you are the perfect super parents while you are totally overwhelmed, can only result in the wasted emotion of self-pity and even more stress. Successful couples grab "the bull by the horns" and work for solutions—recognizing that running a household is not easy. Making a family work is, clearly, difficult even in the best of

times and even more challenging when you are the caring for your children.

5. ***Enhance your love relationship by providing each other occasional time for privacy and aloneness.*** The recognition of the absolute need for privacy and aloneness is, in our judgment after analyzing thousands of interviews, critical to successful marriages. The amount of time available to satisfy these two needs varies from one marriage to another and from one marriage partner to another, and can increase during times of stress. We live such hectic lives at work, at home and when raising children that the time to be alone with our own thoughts is paramount to our ability to engage in meaningful communication with each other. The quality of communication can only be enhanced between the two of you after refreshing your mind and spirit with alone time. You have to belong to yourself before you can belong to others. Unfortunately, moms spend so much time caring for others that they don't take care of their own needs. You can't take good care of others if you don't take good care of yourself.

You brought your children into this world with the greatest of love and now you have to balance all of the stresses they bring to your marriage. Your children won't be with your forever, so enjoy them while you can. Believe it or not they grow up oh so quickly. Cherish those precious moments but remember—*the quality of the relationship between mom and dad trumps everything else.*

Ten Tips for Couples with Special Needs Children

Raising children with special needs can severely challenge your marriage.

*L*IFE IS NOT ALWAYS FAIR, just, and beautiful. Sometimes life doesn't turn out as you had expected. But the truth is, when you are dealt a bad hand, you pick yourself up, dust yourself off, and get back in the game. Giving up, feeling sorry for yourself, and crying over the unfairness of it all, doesn't cut it. Parents of special needs children know this to be true.

Raising children with special needs can severely challenge your marriage. But here is the truth—you cannot let your child's disability or ailment interfere or destroy your marital relationship. As we always say, "The parent's relationship with each other trumps everything else!"

Here are the ten tips for nurturing your marriage while caring for a special needs child:

1. ***Talk openly with each other about feelings, emotions and stresses as they relate to the care of your special needs child.*** In times of stress the tendency is to keep everything bottled up inside or explode over the slightest disagreement. However, this approach will not work if you want your

marriage to survive and thrive. In successful marriages there are No Sacred Cows. They share insights about everything—the good, the bad and the ugly. They are each other's best friends.

2. ***Make a concerted effort to keep the flame of your love affair alive with each other everyday.*** Can you rattle off a list of activities, topics and places you and your spouse include in your personal book of fun and romance? Have you found what clears your mind and gives you an unobstructed view of your world together? If you cannot answer these questions easily, you need to start today by carving out time to have a romantic date with each other, get a hotel room, go for a long walk together, drink a bottle of wine watching the sunset, write a love note, and snuggle in bed a little longer in the morning.

3. ***Approach all financial challenges with teamwork and open communication.*** Balancing the family budget requires teamwork, especially when the added burden of taking care of a special needs child comes your way. It requires common goals. It most certainly requires family support. People in love support each other through thick and thin—through tough times and uncertainty.

4. ***Don't blame each other when things get tough, as casting blame never solved a problem.*** The blame game doesn't work in love and marriage and it is destructive. There is a natural tendency in tough times to blame the one you love for your collective misfortune, but people in love don't blame, castigate, or chastise each other in challenging times.

5. ***Don't wallow in self-pity; it is a wasted emotion.*** No problem has ever been solved by feeling sorry for yourself or your situation. Successful couples grab "the bull by the horns" and work for solutions.

6. *Enhance your love relationship by providing each other occasional time for privacy and aloneness.* The recognition of the absolute need for privacy and aloneness is, in our judgment after analyzing thousands of interviews, critical to successful marriages. The quality of communication can only be enhanced between the two of you after refreshing your mind and spirit with alone time. You have to belong to yourself before you can belong to others.

7. *Remember that in marriage simple things matter and they need to be practiced each day.* Thirty years of research on successful love and marriage has taught us many things, but first and foremost—no love has blossomed or been sustained without doing the simple things. Too often when we are engaged in stressful life altering situations we forget to do the simple things for the one we love the most. If you would like to know more about the simple things that matter in love and marriage read, *Building a Love that Lasts.*

8. *Develop a network of support from family, friends, and relatives.* You and your spouse do not have to do it all by yourselves. Ask your friends and relatives for help. Solicit support from aunts and uncles. Seek support from your neighbors. Don't be shy about asking for help. Don't be deluded into thinking you can do it alone.

9. *Recognize that the time may very well come when you can no longer care for your special needs child by yourself and will have to turn to professional caregivers*—perhaps an assisted-care or similar facility. Don't consume yourself with guilt if that time comes. At this critical juncture in your child's life someone else may very well provide the best care.

10. *Staying healthy and happy, both physically and mentally, should be the highest priority of both you and your spouse.*

Engage in a daily exercise program. Eat healthy—lots of fruits and vegetables. Take your vitamins! Make sure you both take your own medications on the prescribed schedule. And don't forget your annual physical exams. It is nearly impossible to take care of others when you don't take of yourself.

Make no mistake about it—caring for a special needs child can at times be stressful beyond belief. The negative impact on your marriage can be substantial! But the truth is, the damage can be prevented. Having a solid marriage will allow you to overcome almost all obstacles that come your way in life and in your marriage.

Twelve Ways to Help
Your Spouse Face Surgery

Required surgery can be a traumatic
event for you and your spouse.
Brace yourself—you can make a difference!

*T*HE SAD TRUTH OF the matter is this—human beings get sick from time to time. No great revelation here, but when your doctor or the doctor of your spouse tells you that "surgery is required" it can be traumatic—to both of you! It can definitely ruin your day.

When we get married we promise to love and cherish each other "until death do us part." Those are the traditional marriage vows most all of us recite when we get married.

But the fact of the matter is that sometimes those vows are challenged because your spouse gets sick. Sometimes your spouse actually has a health challenge that can only be fixed by surgery. And let's face it, taking your spouse in for surgery is scary as hell!

Here are TWELVE facts you should consider when surgery becomes part of your life and that of your spouse or lover:

1. *Always remember the first rule of surgery, it is minor"* *surgery if it is performed on someone else.* It's "major" surgery when it is performed on you! Do not under any circumstances minimize the risks involved in surgery, even

so-called minor surgery. Surgery is scary, period! It is often traumatic. Do not minimize your spouse's fear or your own.

2. ***Be an advocate for your lover prior to and following surgery.*** When they have surgery stay with them as much as you can in their hospital room to help bath them, make sure they take their medicine, to monitor their intake of food, etc.

3. ***The greatest risk following surgery is infection.*** Monitor the cleanliness of the room, nightstand, their clothing, and their body. And always remember to brush the hair out of their face, hold their hand, and smile a lot. Smiling helps minimize both fear and pain.

4. ***Recognize going into surgery that there will be both emotional and physical aspects involved in recuperation.*** Do your best to be supportive of them during the important recuperation time. Do your best to perk them up, make them laugh and smile, and keep their mind off of their physical pain and oftentimes poor emotional state due to exhaustion and stress.

5. ***Recognize that you, aside from attending medical personal, will probably be the first person to see your spouse following their surgery.*** Be supportive and put on a happy face. Surgery is not just something the one you love experiences— you both experience it.

6. ***Avoid conflict with your recuperating lover following their surgery.*** The last thing either of you need is anger and argumentation during this period of time. Chill out!

7. ***When you take your spouse home make sure you have prepared their bed and the room they will be staying in.*** They will want to go to their room and settle in without you frantically getting the room prepared. Pre-planning the room arrangements with your spouse will go a long way towards making their homecoming non-stressful and comfortable.

8. Keep in near constant communication with your mate for the week or so following surgery. Your spouse needs to know you care and you need to know from your spouse how you can be supportive.

9. Attend to their needs before and after surgery, but recognize that the sooner they can start taking care of themselves again, the better. A high degree of independence is of paramount importance to most human beings. Respect that need in your spouse.10. The good news is this—most people who undergo surgery come through the ordeal with flying colors. Do not go into surgery with an attitude of, "Woe is me (us)." Surgery usually turns out AOK. Expect the best, but be a realist. Your spouse or lover's physician will do his or her best. They are highly trained and experienced. The odds of getting well following surgery are in your spouse or lover's favor. Put trust in the medical team, particularly your surgeon. Hope for the best.

11. Constantly tell your spouse or lover that you love them. You can never say, "I love you," often enough. Say it frequently as you look your significant other directly in their eyes. You have no idea how much power these three words have when it comes to healing!

12. Every time you are with your spouse or lover give them a big hug. Hugs are amongst the greatest elixirs of life. Hugs are among the best promoters of good health. Never forget that the human touch has healing power beyond belief. When the one you love has surgery, they need your hugs. Hug them a lot!

Surgery isn't fun. Surgery isn't grand or glorious. But the truth is, surgery can save your life and can, at the very least, greatly improve the quality of your life. See surgery as a healing opportunity. Just imagine your life or the life of the one you love without it.

Seven Tips to Eliminate Stress During Holidays

Stress, stress, stress!!!
The holiday season can be among the
most stressful times in a relationship.

*T*HE HOLIDAY SEASON is a time of celebration. It is a time to be with family and friends. It is a time to be with the one you love. The holiday season is not a time for stress!

We have all seen it—the grandest of holiday plans come crashing down with the reality of the situation. You work feverishly cooking a delicious holiday dinner for the extended family, only to be left with a pile of dirty dishes while everyone else retires to watch football. What a bummer!

Stress, stress, stress!!! The holiday season can be among the most stressful times in a relationship—make no mistake about it. The mere thought that some of the "rogue" family members are coming to your home, the high cost of everything, and the preparation time required, are enough to send you into a state of depression. Combat that feeling!

Here are a few tips to help you and your spouse lower your stress level and have the best holiday season ever, in spite of the potential stressors coming your way:

1. *Appreciate the traditions within your family and your spouse's family.* Blend them together in a way that both you and your spouse will cherish and make new memories together. Don't feel compelled to follow the exact same traditions of one family over the other without a full discussion of what you both want to create yourselves.

2. *Money is not the solution to a great holiday season—especially in tough economic times.* Rather, it is the simple things that matter—simple acts of kindness, homemade gifts and cards, simple expressions of love.

3. *Talk about what you are going to do for the season—what are you and your spouse's highest priorities?* Have this conversation as soon as possible so you both can feel good about your plans. Then, let all the other holiday "stuff" go by the wayside.

4. *Take a moment in the midst of the chaos and pressure of the holidays to focus on what really matters.* Give your spouse your respect, your understanding, your embrace, your kiss and your time. Don't let the relatives and friends put a wedge between you and the one you love because of the stress and circumstances surrounding the holidays.

5. *When holiday problems arise—as they always do—an open discussion with your spouse needs to happen as soon as possible.* Discussions about serious matters must always begin with agreement about what the issues really are. Work to identify the issue, establish the parameters of the discussion, with agreement to solve the problem together.

6. As the stress rises, so does the opportunity for argument and disagreement. When the holiday tension is so thick that you could cut it with a knife, it is easy to let nasty statements and sharp words roll off your tongue, making judgmental statements about your spouse, their actions, or their friends and relatives. Think twice before exploding with vitriolic words that cannot be taken back.

7. The holiday season doesn't have to be perfect! It is more important to build memories together for the holidays. Invite the family and friends to share in the dinner preparation and holiday decorating. The relationships built are more important than holiday perfection.

Our final thought for the holidays is this—no love has blossomed or been sustained without doing the simple things. Simple things do matter, especially during the holiday season!

Is There Really a
Seven-Year Itch in Marriage?

*It takes character to avoid
the seven-year itch.*

CCORDING TO THE
available research evidence, there
are several periods in a marriage that seem, on average, to be particularly troublesome—the first year, the seventh year, the fifteenth
year, and the 30th year. Marriages that survive and thrive beyond
30 years have virtually no chance of ending in divorce!

Our focus in this article is the *Seven-Year Itch,* so widely
reported in the popular media. Data from the U.S. Census Bureau
would suggest that the *Seven-Year Itch* is, in fact, real.

Some of the most interesting facts about marriage and divorce
have come from the U.S. Census Bureau. Several years ago, the
Census Bureau issued a press release entitled *"Most People Make
Only One Trip Down the Aisle, But First Marriages Shorter."* The fact
reported in the press release that piqued our interest the most was:
"On average, first marriages that end in divorce last about eight
years." This is the phenomenon often called the *"Seven-Year Itch."*

First, a little background. Most aficionados of the *Seven-Year
Itch* trace it back to a play by the same name written by one George
Axelrod. His three-act play was first performed on Broadway in
New York City in 1952. Three years later, a movie by the same title

starring the late, great Marylyn Monroe was released by 20th Century Fox.

Before we get to the "plot" of this article, we also wanted to remind you that the *Seven-Year Itch* has also been associated with an itchy and irritating skin rash that has been reported to last for up to seven years. Frankly, this notion is very closely related to what happens in a number of marriages as we explain in the paragraphs to follow.

In the most basic sense, the *Seven-Year Itch* is the inclination of some to become unfaithful to their spouse after seven years of marriage. In the play and the movie of the same title, a married man by the name of Richard is currently reading a book about to be published by his company entitled *"7-Year Itch."* The book offers the notion that a large percentage of men have extra-marital affairs after seven years of marriage; hence, the *Seven-Year Itch.* At the same time he is reading the book, he meets a young blond television model. As you might imagine, the plot thickens!

The more basic question is, how do you stay faithful to the one you love and keep your loving relationship healthy and strong so it survives. **We offer these seven tips to help you avoid the *Seven-Year Itch*:**

1. *Understand that the occasional temptation to betray the trust of the one you love through infatuation with another person is a perfectly normal feeling* when it comes to love and marriage. Being infatuated with another person doesn't make you less human. Accept that these feelings are natural.

2. *Actually acting on the feelings of infatuation and temptation impulses is not normal and destroys the underlying foundation of a marriage.* Take time to fully think through the consequences before you make that choice. There is no mistake about it, cheating on your spouse is deadly to the trust in your relationship.

3. *Recognize that continuing and recurring fantasies and infatuations about another person is a strong indicator* of something amiss in your relationship with your spouse.

4. *The "turn the corner rule"—is to address the issue head-on with your loving partner.* Failure to do so will doom your relationship to the ash-heap of lost love.

5. *Love takes hard work.* Frankly, sometimes you determine that your loving relationship is lost. But more likely, you discover that you truly love your spouse. You must save this relationship by committing to the hard work it will take to rebuild the love.

6. *Seek help!* Sometimes couples turn to a marriage counselor. Others learn how to make their relationship work by reading what others, including us, have discovered. You can learn so much about your relationship by "discovering" what others have already learned!

7. *Sometimes you have to "fish or cut bait."* The reality is that some marriages cannot be saved. But hopefully an examination will reveal your relationship is worth saving. You should always work towards that end if you are to avoid the *Seven-Year Itch.*

As the Census data suggest, there just might be something to the *Seven-Year Itch* when it comes to marriage. The more basic question is, how do you stay faithful to the one you love and keep your loving relationship healthy and strong so it survives the ups, the downs, and the temptations present in all relationships at one time or another.

Can Your Marriage Survive Bullying?

 *Love by bullying never works.*

*B*E STRONG. Be brave. Never succumb to a bully, even if it is someone you love deeply. To do so diminishes the value of your relationship, forever. You simply cannot live with being bullied.

A bully tries to get what they want by intimidating you and by making you feel inferior to them. This should NEVER work! Yet, so many good folks succumb to the bully—and we wonder why.

So what is a bully? In the simplest terms, a bully is someone who can't get what he or she wants through normal means. What they want is power. When you deny them that power they can resort to forceful means to get what they want.

Here is how bullying works in love and marriage. One of the folks in the relationship wants something—be it a new car, a new apartment, a new dishwasher, or a new toy of some variety. The other person involved in the relationship does not. As you might guess, all heck breaks loose!

The bully in the relationship must get what he or she wants. So instead of acting rationally (i.e., Do we have enough money to pay for this?), the bully resorts to name-calling ("You are a hateful person for always keeping me from buying things!"), intimidation ("If you don't let me buy this I am walking out the door."), or they resort to making you feel inferior ("How could someone like you be so stupid?").

Peace or turmoil? If you are like most people, you would rather have peace. So, in the interest of maintaining harmony in your relationship, you fall prey to the bullying. You give them what they want.

But here is the deal—this strategy never works! You give them what they want and they then do it to you again! You always succumb to their wishes. You always lose. Letting them win is a bad idea.

Truth is, real loving relationships are not about you and me. A loving relationship is about US! It is about WE. It does take two to Tango. You cannot Tango by yourself. Until you learn this important relationship lesson, your relationship will be doomed to failure. Finding the courage to stand up to a bully is perhaps the only way to effectively stop the bullying.

So, how do you handle the bully in your relationship?

The answer in a nutshell is, never succumb to their wishes when they resort to bullying. Keep your composure. Be strong!

The simple truth is, bullies should never be allowed to win—even if the bully is your lover or spouse. True loving relationships are about making important decisions together. Once you fall into the trap of allowing yourself to be intimidated or bullied, your relationship is headed for an irreversible demise. Rarely does a relationship recover from this.

There is NO place for bullying in any relationship. It is NOT something you can live with. This is among the most important lessons of love and of life. Learn this lesson well.

Is Infidelity a Deal Breaker?

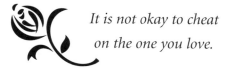

*It is not okay to cheat
on the one you love.*

CHEATING ON A
spouse is the ultimate form of betrayal. It destroys trust, which is at
the very core of any loving relationship.

It is not okay to cheat on the one you love and let's quit pretending that it is. Enough is enough! Character in love and marriage
matters.

We have been reminded again and again that trust is at the very
heart of all successful and long-lasting relationships between people
who love each other.

The essence of our message is this—trust undergirds everything
in a successful marriage and the violation of that trust—the
betrayal of that trust—will, in the end, ruin most marriages that
experience it. Think about it, is there a worst sin that a spouse could
commit than to betray the trust and the sacred honor of their
marriage—of their relationship with the one they purport to love?
And the plain and simple fact is this—most marriages NEVER
recover from this level of trauma to the relationship.

Don't kid yourself, when you make the decision to cheat on your
spouse, you have made a decision that will almost always cause

irreparable harm to your loving relationship—one from which your marriage and your family will never recover.

In our more than 37 years of marriage research on all seven continents of the world, we have rarely observed couples that rebuilt their relationship following infidelity. Those who suggest otherwise are delusional!

By definition, those who engage in infidelity are dishonest, disloyal, and possess an absence of moral fortitude within the relationship, so rebuilding the trust is an almost insurmountable obstacle. Simply put, being unfaithful to your spouse is not conducive to a wholesome, successful, and endearing relationship. Infidelity destroys most relationships where it is present, make no mistake about that.

Over the years, we have interviewed a lot of people who are deeply in love. We have interviewed thousands of couples that repeated the vows, "Until Death Do Us Part." And these are not just words! To love someone for a lifetime does not occur by accident. To be in love is not an accident. To be in love is to do the simple things day in and day out of your relationship with the one you say you love. In other words, you cannot betray the one you love and expect your marriage or relationship to survive and thrive.

It pains our heart to see couples espouse the virtues of the "Desperate Housewives," thinking it's okay to cheat on a loved one and everything will be okay. It drives an arrow through our hearts to think that there are people engaged in a loving relationship who think that betrayal is an offense for which there is forgiveness.

The ultimate betrayal of the one you say you love is an unrecoverable act! Writers, therapists, counselors, and psychologists who suggest otherwise are not only fooling themselves, they are misleading those they purport to want to help. There is rarely EVER a recovery from a relationship that sinks to cheating, betrayal, infidelity, and disloyalty. Those who have been successfully married for years know this to be true. Don't be misled by those who suggest otherwise.

There are lots of articles on the Internet that suggest infidelity is an epidemic in the USA. Some of the Internet pundits even suggest that over 50% of people in a marriage cheat, while others state that it is as high as 70% for men. Both of these notions are completely ludicrous!

In fact, infidelity in the USA has NOT increased in more than 20 years! Moreover, the best available evidence from our own three decades of marriage research, as well as the findings of other well-respected marriage researchers in the country, concludes that fewer than five percent of men and three percent of women are unfaithful on a yearly basis.

W. Bradford Wilcox, Ph.D., Director of the highly respected *Marriage Project* at the University of Virginia, notes that 22% percent of men who have ever been married and 14% of women who have ever been married, had an extra-marital affair over the course of their lifetime.

It is our considered opinion, the notion of character in marriage is real. To suggest otherwise is to ignore the basic tenets of successful relationships. Being honest and trustworthy is at the heart of all the best loving relationships we have studied. These couples trust each other with their lives, their fortunes and their sacred honor. The damage done by breaking that trust it just too great. The relationship will never be the same.

We guess that it is time to say, "The buck stops here!" This is not an issue that you can equivocate about. Infidelity is definitely a deal-breaker!

There are NO excuses for infidelity! There is no way to excuse infidelity or to accept it. It is a deal breaker—first time, second time, anytime! Cheating on the one you love is the most unpardonable of all sins. When a spouse or lover violates the "core of trust" or the "bond of faith" in the relationship, the very foundation of that relationship has likely been destroyed. Rebuilding the trust after an affair is an almost insurmountable obstacle.

Infidelity in a marriage is an unrecoverable act for most who engage in such actions. But let's face it, having so many Internet pundits OVERSTATE the extent of infidelity serves NO useful purpose. It's time folks who write about marriage start speaking the truth. It's that simple.

In life and love, the simple things matter, and the simple truth is, violating the most sacred of all trusts between two human beings who love each other is the ultimate betrayal. Think about this before you cheat on your spouse, before you commit your love to another human being, and before you say "I do."

Character in marriage matters!

Is Your Pooch
Enhancing Your Marriage?

There are several ways a dog
can enhance or
interfere with your relationship.

*S*UCCESSFULLY MARRIED couples often tell us that dogs enhance their love and make them feel more secure in their relationship. In fact, the thousands of happily married couples we have interviewed over the past 37 years are more likely to have dogs than not.

Those happily married couples with dogs report that their dogs enhance their relationship in four ways:

1. *There is a genuine connection between the pet and their owner.* Most married couples with dogs consider their pooch a member of the family and have learned how to tend to their pooch's needs and visa-versa. This is a process that strengthens a love relationship.

2. *The amazing healing power of dogs has been well documented.* It is especially powerful when people are physically ill, injured, lonely, or depressed. Intuitively, dogs provide their owners with soothing calmness in times of stress, comfort in times of sadness, and companionship in times of loneliness.

3. *A dog loves you unconditionally.* A dog doesn't love you "If you do something he likes," "If you feed him," "If you let him

sleep with you in bed," "If you comb his fur," or "If you take him to the vet." He just loves you unconditionally. People in relationships should learn this simple lesson from dogs.

4. A dog is always faithful. No matter what the circumstances, you can always count on your dog to remain a faithful companion. If humans showed this same loyalty to each other, they would be one step closer to having a successful lifelong, loving relationship.

While dogs can enhance the relationships of newly married couples, those four-legged friends can also interfere with the relationship. **There are four ways a dog can interfere with your new marriage:**

1. *You love your dog obsessively.* Doting on your pooch and his needs instead of fostering your new marriage can interfere with building the deep bonds needed for a lasting love.

2. *A pooch can ruin your sex life.* You love your pooch to pieces but when a 100-pound Golden Retriever wants to get in bed between you, it definitely hampers your romantic inclinations.

3. *Your dog may get jealous of the intentions of your new husband/wife.* Avoid being overly concerned with the jealous reactions of your dog. Instead, encourage your new spouse to lavish attention on your pooch, so it doesn't feel slighted and looks forward to the extra attention that comes when your new partner is with you.

4. *Your new husband/wife doesn't like your dog.* It becomes a definite problem if your new husband/wife starts picking on your dog by pushing or kicking your dog away and stating, "Get away from me, you're messing up my pants." Trying to have a serious lasting relationship with a non-dog lover can create enormous challenges. Remember, dogs have an intu-

itive sense about people and a unique ability to them. It goes without saying that a serious discussion about the place of a dog or dogs in your marriage should occur well before you get married.

Many dog owners in search of true love want to find a mate who is a dog lover as well. Pets can serve as important sources of social and emotional support, so it's usually a deal breaker if the other person doesn't like or get along with your dog.

It's important to observe how your new spouse treats and talks to dogs that are not yours. A true dog lover will treat all dogs with respect and love, not just your dog because he or she wants to win you over!

If you are a dog lover, we hope you have found the love of your life, who also loves the dog in your life. If you have, your life will be greatly enhanced.

'Deadwalking' Kills Relationships - Three Ways to Kick the Habit

So whether you are Deadwalking or Pphubbing, there are potential dangers to you and your love life.

*W*HILE WE HAVE ALL heard about the dangers to you of being distracted by your Smart Phone, there is a recent Baylor University study (Roberts and David, 2015) that reveals Pphubbing ("partner phone snubbing") is actually dangerous to your relationship.

According to Roberts and David, Pphubbing is the extent to which people use or are distracted by their mobile devices while in the company of their relationship partners. When you or your partner are constantly distracted by your respective cell phones during a conversation, great harm can occur to your relationship with each other according to the researchers. For example, Pphubbing can lead to depression by one or both of you, decrease the level of satisfaction with your romantic relationship, interfere with your personal sense of well-being, and at times, make one or both of you angry or jealous of each other over the lack of personal attention being paid to each other.

In a recent article, constantly distracted smart phone users, or "Zombie-like" creatures, were referred to as "Deadwalkers." Can being one of these "Deadwalkers" cause danger to you personally?

We have all seen people texting and talking on the phone while jogging. People send text messages or email while on escalators, while driving, while working, and the list goes on. How many people have walked in front of your car while you are making a right turn because they are too preoccupied with their hand-held device?

Of course, the great dangers of "Deadwalking" are clear and the Internet, newspapers, and other sources tell us daily stories about people who got hit while staring zombie-like at their mobile device, who wrecked their car while texting, and who got hurt at work because they were preoccupied with their smart phone.

So whether you are Deadwalking or Pphubbing, there are potential dangers to you and your love life. We first wrote about the negative impact Smart Phones can have on your love life nearly a decade ago. And the truth is, it seems the problems associated with the distraction from these devices has only gotten worse.

So, how do you keep yourself from the "crack" addiction to your Smart Phone? Here are three strategies that can help you begin the withdrawal process:

1. ***Turn off alerts:*** Alerts are the first interruption to your relationship. Instead of concentrating on the one you love, you are distracted by the constant dinging of the phone. Natural curiosity takes over when you hear the ding and you just have to check what just came in. Turning off the alert system is the first step in you taking control of the urge to get on your Smart Phone.

2. ***Put your phone out of reach when having a conversation:*** You just cannot have a good conversation if you are not paying close attention to each other. A conversation with the one you love is more important than being distracted by your Smart Phone. Put your Smart Phone down and pay attention to the one you love.

3. Check your phone only at certain times: Determine if you are going to check your phone once an hour or every two hours. Since messages are asynchronous (are not in real time), you can delay your response. The conversation and attention to the one you love is in real time, which is adversely effected by Pphubbing or Deadwalking.

Remember our constant refrain regarding successful loving relationships, "Love is simple to understand. The problem is people won't do the simple things required to make love work." The Smart Phone is a perfect example. Being constantly distracted by your Smart Phone is one of the fastest ways to destroy your relationship. While it is a simple thing, you have to work hard to withdrawal from Pphubbing or Deadwalking.

We notice many couples using their Smart Phones as they walked with each other. And they weren't talking to each other! Like most things in life, there is a time and place for the Smart Phone. The time you spend together is precious. Walking and talking is one of the best things couples can do for their relationship. Leave the Smart Phone at home when you spend those moments. Save the Smart Phone for the times you are alone. Your relationship and your love will thank you for it.

Those great marriages we write about are often achieved as a result of lots of walking and talking together! Maybe we will see you on one of those walks. Without the Smart Phones of course!

Love by Dancing

A great relationship can be improved by simple acts. Just go dancing!

A TEXAS FRIEND OF OURS swears that great love comes to those who dance. And guess what, he makes a very compelling case!

In a nutshell, we have concluded that one of the seven secrets of a successful loving relationship is touching. If you pass the one you love 100 times a day, touch them! Touching acknowledges the presence of the one you love and tells them, "I love you so much I simply must touch you."

We base this finding about "touching" on our study of 20,000 years of successful marriage—marriages we studied across cultures and continents, across ethnicities, and across the socio-economic spectrum. Touching is a very important part of love. All successful loving relationships thrive on the human touch by the one they love and the one who loves them.

Dancing is a great example of touching. We have written endlessly about the Tango, a dance we call the "dance of love." When we traveled to Buenos Aires, Argentina recently we were blown away by the exotic and loving nature of the Tango. They dance it on the street, in Tango clubs like *Senor Tango,* and at home! In fact, we were so enamored with the Tango, we wrote a chapter in our book about it entitled "It Takes Two To Tango."

Now, here is where this all comes together. The great marriages and loving relationships we have studied demonstrate the power of touch in the loving relationship. Relationships that touch the most, *love the most.* We are convinced of that!

And secondly, we are absolutely convinced of this important axiom—it takes two to Tango. You cannot Tango by yourself. In so many ways, the Tango is the essence of so many successful loving relationships. In the best marriages and loving relationships we have studied, "I" and "me" and "you" becomes "we" and "us" and "our."

So you now see why dancing is such a great way to find love, to be in love, and to enjoy love. Our Texas friend is a smart guy!

Every loving relationships hits bumps in the road. Sometimes those bumps turn into earthquakes! The point is, even the best relationships have moments when they hit a wall—when they are full of despair and angst. In our opinion, based on years of research and observation, these periods strengthen these relationships. Do not despair!

Here is what you do next time your relationship is down and when your relationship has lost some of its romance—go dancing! Whatever your favorite music venue is, find it and go dancing. Whether it is Big Band, Tango, Country Dancing, Samba, the Cha Cha, Disco, Waltz, Swing, or the Salsa, *just go dancing!* You will spend the night touching the one you love, sharing wonderful and sensual moments together, and regaining once again the magic of why you are in love because it does take Two to Tango.

Ah, Love by Dancing—is there anything better? And as we always say, in love and marriage the simple things matter. A great relationship can be improved by simple acts. Just go dancing!

Don't Let Negative Intruders Destroy Your Marriage

Always remember that the relationship between husband and wife trumps everything else.

THERE ARE SERIOUS consequences to your personal mental health and the relationship with your spouse when you let negativity impact your life. The steady drumbeat of bad news in your newspaper; the bombardment of negativity on the Internet, television, and radio; the intrusion of others and the constant negative exchanges you have on social media—much of it from your "so-called friends"—is enough to make you want to crawl in a hole and hide!

If you spend too much of your day being told how awful everything is, it WILL affect the way you feel, the way you relate to others—especially the one you love—and the way you love. You see, getting in the doldrums—letting your psychic be impacted in negative ways by the constant negativity from interference and intrusions—can begin to bring you down and affect your marriage in terrible and unproductive ways.

So, how do you prevent and combat the daily bombardment of the negative intruders in your life and the negative things you experience? How do you keep negativity from affecting your relationships with those you love, especially your spouse?

We have discovered five effective solutions to protect you and your marriage from intruders based on our 37 years of research with successfully married couples in 55 countries on all seven continents of the world. **Here are the five solutions in a nutshell:**

1. ***Determine who the intruders are that adversely affect your relationship with each other.*** Here are some categories to consider:

   • Family members who want to interfere with the lives of you and your spouse. They constantly infer that you are not doing things correctly, they know better than you and your spouse, and they are always there with unwanted advice about how you should do things differently.

   • Friends who do not have your best interests in mind. They sap the joy out of your relationship for their own satisfaction. They are negative people who cannot find beauty or pleasure in your happiness. Negativity can bring you and your spouse down.

   • People who are only interested in feathering their own nest. They want to emotionally leach off of you and your spouse. They make you feel guilty for being successful and happy in your marriage. These are the worst kind of toxic people! They undermine your relationships in so many ways.

   • Social media "friends" who play the one-upmanship games by putting you down, treading on your successes and bringing negative thoughts into your world. With social media there is a tendency to pick up all "friend" requests, even if they are not people you want or need in your circle. Determine which social media friends have a positive impact and which friends spend much of their time putting you down, criticizing you, making fun of you, or embarrassing you in front of others. Eliminating negative people from your life is an essential step in achieving an emotional healthy marriage.

- Adult children who cause trouble by bringing a steady stream of consternation and interference to your relationship. Adult children can adversely impact the relationship between their parents by trying to be an unneeded and unwanted confidant and advice giver, becoming a source for wasted and unnecessary arguments, or by presenting their constant needs to you for resolution. Too many older couples blame themselves for their children's bad behavior or mistakes. Unfortunately, couples take too much responsibility for the good and way too much responsibility for the bad. School, everyday life, college, work and friends have much more influence on how children turn out than their parents.

- Daily bad news coming from television, newspapers, Internet or news feeds can be an intrusion upon you and your relationship. Let's face it—the world is a mess at times. When confronted constantly with the realities of terrorism, damaging weather events, financial crisis, government issues, and tragic deaths, it can put you in the doldrums. Letting your psychic be impacted in negative ways by the intrusion of negativity in the news and in social media can affect your marital relationship in terrible and unproductive ways.

- Work, organizations, children's activities and sports can all be intruders upon the time and commitment each of you invest into your relationship. The lack of time to building a strong friendship with each other can be adversely affected by the demands of work, organizational memberships, children's activities, hobbies, or sports. Learning to limit the impact of these intruders is critical to a successful relationship.

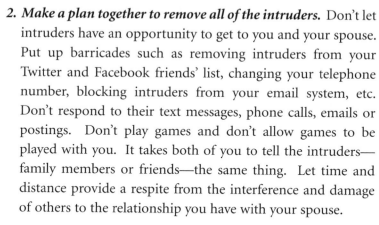
2. Make a plan together to remove all of the intruders. Don't let intruders have an opportunity to get to you and your spouse. Put up barricades such as removing intruders from your Twitter and Facebook friends' list, changing your telephone number, blocking intruders from your email system, etc. Don't respond to their text messages, phone calls, emails or postings. Don't play games and don't allow games to be played with you. It takes both of you to tell the intruders—family members or friends—the same thing. Let time and distance provide a respite from the interference and damage of others to the relationship you have with your spouse.

3. Place time limits on the intrusions from all outside sources. Agree to limit on a daily basis the amount of news you watch, read in the newspaper, and consume from the Internet, so you can focus positive energy on your relationship. Be informed, but enough is enough! Help each other manage the excessive time commitments from after hours work assignments, children's activities, hobbies, sports, and organizations. Building a lasting love takes quality time with each other. Anything that enters into the boundary of your relationship needs to be carefully thought through and managed.

4. Make your number one priority nurturing the relationship between you and your spouse. That means bringing your problems to each other to solve, not confiding in a family member or friend who is an intruder in the friendship you have with your spouse. When you bring your problems to others instead of your spouse, you put a wedge in the bond you have with each other.

5. Everyday of your life do something positive for the one you love! When you engage in acts of kindness, make compliments and say nice things to your spouse, you are enhancing the strength of the boundary the two of you have established to keep intruders out. It takes daily work to keep a relationship positive with an often-time negative world whirling around you. There is one simple rule of the Universe—a smile requires fewer muscles than a frown. Be a positive person. You will be astonished at how much better the world will seem AND become! It can even change the way your spouse feels about your marriage if he or she is greeted with daily acts of kindness and a positive attitude.

Always remember that the relationship between husband and wife trumps everything else. Using these five solutions will help you protect your marriage from the negative affects of intruders and intrusions. Only then can you find true happiness with each other and build a lasting love.

Good Sex Will Not
Save Your Marriage

*To single out sex is to blow its importance
entirely out of proportion to its
relevance to a great marriage.*

OH MY GOODNESS, WHAT NEXT?
We heard today that a minister in Grapevine, Texas once told his congregation in his sermon that he wanted married couples to have sex all week long! He said that God may have rested on the seventh day, but he wanted married couples to have sex every day for a week!

He went on to say, "I won't be dressed in pajamas" while delivering his sermon sitting on a bed. In these days of financial crisis, debates over same-sex marriage, and the like, it's time, he says, to turn the "whining" into "whoopee."

The question is, where do you start with debunking such a ridiculous notion. Let us count the ways!

For starters, we all know that good sex can be fun, romantic, exciting, and something that makes most consenting adults feel warm and fuzzy all over. Over the years we have interviewed thousands of successfully married couples and most report a reasonable degree of satisfaction with their sex life. But here is our most important research finding concerning this issue—no marriage was ever saved or made successful because the couple had a great sex life!

And more importantly, when we ask successfully married couples how important sex is to the success of their marriage—to rank on a scale of 1-10 with 10 high—the average rank over the years has been 6. This finding has held true over the 37 years of our research. That's hardly a resounding endorsement for the importance of sex in a marriage.

You see, marriage is a multi-faceted relationship, and in the best marriages no one aspect stands out as the make or break part of it. The truth is, and as we have reported in several of our books and over 1000 articles, there are seven pervasive characteristics present in all successful marriages. And guess what, sex is not one of them!

As we say so often in our many interviews and writings, all of the married couples representing the best marriages we have interviewed have shared with us the importance of touching in their relationship. One gentleman we interviewed told us that if he passed his wife in the house a hundred times a day, he touched her. To touch someone you love is to acknowledge their presence and to communicate your love for them. That's why the most successfully married couples amongst us do it so often.

In our humble opinion, the minister's charge to his congregation to have sex seven days next week not only cheapens the importance of healthy and positive sex with someone you love, but it also reinforces the silliness that great sex will save your marriage—that sex is the centerpiece of all good marriages.

As you know from our many writings, we believe that the overemphasis on sex in books about love and marriage cause people to believe that if they don't have stupendous sex everyday there is something wrong with their marriage. Trust us on this—marriages that fail do so for a variety of reasons and not for a *single* reason.

We are sure the good Reverend was well intentioned with his challenge to his congregation, but we believe his advice was misguided as it once again overemphasizes the importance of sex in marriage. To single out sex is to blow its importance entirely out of proportion to its relevance to a great marriage. We wish people would stop doing that!

We reported many first hand accounts from successfully married couples who emphasized how important the human touch is to a loving marriage. They hug each other often, they kiss, they touch each other while talking, they sit cheek to cheek on the couch while having a conversation, they curl around each other when they sleep or just gaze at the stars, and yes, they have sex from time to time—when it's right for them and not forced by some arbitrary "have sex everyday rule!"

You see, people touch each other in many, many different ways and no single form of touching wins the day. It's what we like to call "the accumulation of touching" that matters. Touch the one you love often and in whatever gentle way your heart desires. It's that human connection that wins the day—and wins the marriage! The simple truth is, the best marriages engage in a lot of touching, sex is only one of them.

Touch well! Love well!

Aging Parents Can Stress Your Marriage

Our research over the years suggests that there are a number of useful tips that you can use to not only deal with the stress of caregiving, but also strengthen your marriage at the same time.

WE ARE "BABY-BOOMERS." Like some 80 million Americans, we were born during the period 1946-1964. We are that generation of Americans born to what former NBC anchor Tom Brokaw called, "The Greatest Generation." Our parents survived the Great Depression, won the Second World War, and by most accounts, saved the world and preserved democracy in a post-war era.

There is no doubt; the free world owes a great debt of gratitude to the Greatest Generation. Frankly, it is hard to imagine where we would be without their sacrifices and their contributions to the creation of modern day America—to the creation of the world we live in today. We owe our parents a lot; there is no doubt about that.

Like some of you, our parents are gone. Losing our respective parents was among the most difficult things we have had to cope with in our lives. But the undeniable truth of life is this—you will not get out of this world alive!

As we write this for you today, we are fully cognizant that the parents of the baby-boomers are dying by the hundreds everyday. People get old and they die. There is nothing mysterious going on here. The realities of life tell us that the inevitable is lurking on the horizon. But the good news, our parents are living longer and longer. We get to have them around for a greater portion of our lives than our parents had of their parents.

Having aging parents who might live into their 80's and 90's (and beyond) can, however, bring a whole new set of challenges to your own marriage. You will recall the challenges associated with having children enter your own marriage. Nora Ephron once said that having children was "like throwing a hand grenade into a marriage!" Having your aging parents move back into your marriage, whether in your home or theirs, can have much the same effect.

When you take on the responsibility of caring for aging parents you will, without a doubt, take on some enormous stresses. The many challenges of caring for aging parents will at times put unbelievable strain on your marital relationship. Our research over the years suggests that there are a number of useful tips that you can use to not only deal with the stress of caregiving, but also strengthen your marriage at the same time.

Tips for Caregivers to Strengthen Your Marriage:

1. ***Talk openly with each other about feelings, emotions and stresses as they relate to your care of aging parents.*** In times of stress the tendency is to keep everything bottled up inside or explode with the slightest disagreement. However, this approach will not work if you want your marriage to survive and thrive. In successful marriages there are *No Sacred Cows*. Simply speaking, happily married couples talk about every-

thing. All subjects are fair game. They trust each other. They rely on each other's good judgment. They depend upon each other for truth and straight talk. They share insights about everything —the good, the bad and the ugly. They are each other's best friends.

2. Approach all financial challenges with teamwork and open communication. Balancing the family budget requires teamwork, especially when the added burden of taking care of aging parents comes your way. It requires common goals. It most certainly requires family support. People in love support each other through thick and thin—through tough times and uncertainty. The unequivocal truth is this—if you don't view your relationship as one requiring teamwork, all is lost. If you don't work together to address head-on the economic challenges of your relationship with each other when caring for an aging parent, there is little hope of success.

3. Don't blame each other when things get tough, as casting blame never solved a problem. The blame game doesn't work in love and marriage and it is destructive. There is a natural tendency in tough times to blame the one you love for your collective misfortune, but people in love don't blame, castigate, or chastise each other in challenging times. The truth is, there usually is no one to blame for the situation. Someone has to take care of aging parents and the job just fell to you.

4. Don't wallow in self-pity; it is a wasted emotion. No problem has ever been solved by feeling sorry for yourself or your situation. Successful couples grab "the bull by the horns" and work for solutions—recognizing that running a household is not easy. Making a family work is, clearly, difficult even in the best of times and even more challenging when you are the caregiver for an aging parent.

5. **Make a concerted effort to keep the flame of your love affair alive with each other everyday.** Can you rattle off a list of activities, topics and places that you and your spouse include in your personal book of fun and romance? Have you found what clears your mind and gives you an unobstructed view of your world together? What type of priority do you place on making time for fun and romance with each other in your hectic lives? If you cannot answer these questions easily, you need to start today with carving out time to have a romantic date with each other, bring home flowers, get a hotel room, go for a long walk together, drink a bottle of wine watching the sunset, write a love note, and snuggle in bed a little longer.

6. **Enhance your love relationship by providing each other occasional time for privacy and aloneness.** The recognition of the absolute need for privacy and aloneness is, in our judgment after analyzing thousands of interviews, critical to successful marriages. The amount of time available to satisfy these two needs varies from one marriage to another and from one marriage partner to another, and can increase during times of stress. We live such hectic lives at work, at home and when caring for aging parents that the time to be alone with our own thoughts is paramount to our ability to engage in any meaningful communication. The quality of communication can only be enhanced between the two of you after refreshing your mind and spirit with alone time. You have to belong to yourself before you can belong to others.

7. **Remember that the "Simple Things Matter" in marriage and they need to be practiced each day.** Thirty-seven years of research on successful love and marriage has taught us many things, but first and foremost—no love has blossomed or been sustained without doing the "simple things." Big things

don't matter until your relationship has mastered the art of doing the simple things day in and day out in your relationship with another human being whom you purport to love. Too often when we are engaged in stressful life altering situations such as caring for aging parents we forget to just do the "simple things" for the one we love the most. Try engaging in simple acts of kindness, always treating each other with courtesy, sharing a shower together, and hugging often. Trust us on this—if your relationship with the one you love has mastered the art of doing the simple things day in and day out, the likelihood of your relationship making it through the tough times are multiplied many times over. The point is, "simple things matter" and when you practice doing them, they accumulate. Simple acts of kindness add up.

Your parents cared for you. They took you through your tough times growing up and, like most parents, probably continued to provide support for you long after you left their home. Like many children of aging parents, it is now your time to return the favor.

Your parents deserve your love, your understanding, and your support in their time of need. Rather than accept this responsibility as a challenge, take it on as an opportunity to get closer to your parents and deepen your love for them. They won't be around forever. Enjoy them while you can.

✍

The Empty Nest Can Be Better Than You Think!

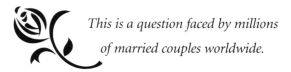

This is a question faced by millions of married couples worldwide.

*L*ET'S FACE IT— the empty nest syndrome is most overrated! The truth is, for many couples, the empty nest is a time of great "re-discovery" of their love for each other.

Okay, the children have all left home. You and your spouse are finally alone after two decades of marriage. Now what? This is a question faced by millions of married couples worldwide.

You get married, your children are born, they grow up, and they leave home. No matter where you live on planet Earth, married couples with children will eventually have to deal with the empty nest.

Here is what we have learned over the past four decades from our thousands of interviews with successfully married couples:

1. ***Empty nesters need to take stock of their relationship now that the children are out of the house.*** They need to set goals for their relationship and plot a direction they want their marriage to go. Married couples often need to rediscover each other. And if you are lucky, you will spend the rest of

your natural born life with your spouse. The quality of your relationship must be good if your marriage is to survive and thrive—post-children.

2. *If your marriage is typical, the chances are very high that both husband and wife work outside the home.* The great danger for empty nesters is that they often throw themselves even more into their work, often at the expense of their spouse. Your careers are important to you, but plunging your heart and soul into your work as a way of compensating for the absence of children in your home will only cause stress in your relationship with your mate.

3. *Rekindle the romance and passion of your relationship that is often put on the backburner when you are raising children.* Get in the habit again of engaging in passion with each other. You will be surprised at how easy it will be to fall in love all over again with your spouse. Practice, practice, practice!

4. *The health of your spouse is of paramount importance to your marriage, especially in the empty nest.* The two of you should take action to improve and enhance your health. Eat healthy foods, get plenty of exercise, and get annual physical exams. You'll have more energy, be healthier, and live longer!

5. *The final piece of advice goes like this—the worst thing you can do to your spouse or yourself as an empty nester is to hover over each other all the time!* As we have said before, there is a fundamental predisposition in every human being to have time alone. Empty nesters have more time to be together, but couples often forget that the need to be alone is just as strong and just as important when the children are gone

Living in an empty nest is not all that bad. Couples have been doing it for centuries! Follow the simple rules espoused by those

who have been there, done that, and been successful at it. You won't regret it.

Re-discover each other in the "empty nest." If you are like most couples, you will like what you find.

Sustaining Love and Marriage in Retirement

Reinvesting your time in the one you love can bring enormous benefits.

*Y*OU SPENT A LIFETIME together raising children, going to work, going to meetings, and in general, meeting everyone else's needs. Whether one or both of you worked outside of the home, you are now retired, together in the house alone . . . just you and your spouse . . . now what?

If you are among the lucky ones, you will get to retire someday and spend more time with your spouse. Actuarially, a retired couple at age 65 has a reasonable chance of spending two more decades of life together until "death do us part." The question is, how do you make these 20 years together enjoyable, fun and exciting?

We are certainly not interested in being morbid about the prospects of death, but as Charley's mother used to say, "You are not going to get out of this world alive!" The truth is, death is a natural part of life. It is inevitable. So, the question becomes, how do you spend those nearly two decades of life with the one you love doing the things you want to do while free of the burdens and stresses associated with work? This question is one all married couples must ultimately deal with if they are lucky.

In a few weeks we are going to be interviewed about love and marriage in retirement so we have been gleaning a lot information from the many interviews we have conducted over the years with successfully married couples over the age of 65.

We think you will these find the results interesting:

1. *Take the time to get to know each other again when one or both of you retire!* When we first heard this notion years ago we were somewhat taken aback by it. After all, these couples had been married for 30 or more years! Why would they have to get to know each other again? The truth is, the hectic pace of life for so many years—much of it outside the home and family—does change many of the dynamics of the marital relationship. For example, the various responsibilities of running a home, raising children, and the like while one or both work outside the home often change when retirement comes along. And the simple truth is, many of those who retire need to renew many aspects of their loving relationship.

2. *Never wile away your hours together everyday in front of the television!* It's a trap so many fall into when they retire. Take a walk, plan a trip, visit your grandchildren, plant a garden, go dancing—plan activities that keep you active and that you can enjoy together. Becoming a couch potato or a back porch rocker is not good for either you or your spouse. Plan something to do outside the home every day. Stay active. Stay healthy. Stay tuned to events in the world surrounding you. Stay young!

3. *Respect the need for privacy and aloneness in yourself and your spouse.* You will both be better off for it. The worst thing you can do to your spouse or yourself when one or both

of you retire is hover over each other all the time. Just as you need alone time before retirement, you need it after retirement. As you have heard us report in our writings and books, there is a fundamental predisposition in every human being to have time alone. Everybody needs time to be with their own thoughts, with their own hobbies, with just themselves. Being retired may give you more time to be together, but couples often forget that the need to be alone is just as strong and just as important when you retire.

4. **Build a social network of family and friends.** Don't become isolated! And as much as you would like not to believe this, most of the people you worked with will move on with their lives when you retire. You won't hear from most of them again. They are not being mean or cruel to you. It's just the way life is. You will need to make new friends, meet new acquaintances, build new relationships, and establish new social networks.

5. **Be spontaneous with much of your day.** Having unencumbered time is, perhaps, the greatest gift of retirement. Think about it—all those years you worked at a job, raised kids, volunteered—you rarely had unencumbered time. We, like the couples we have interviewed almost four decades of life, have this insatiable need from time to time to plan nothing for the day! In many ways, those are the best days of our lives together as it is for many of the retired couples we have interviewed. Oh, don't get us wrong. Sometimes you have to plan your day, but not everyday!

6. **Never take the health of yourself or your spouse for granted.** The health of a spouse is of profound importance. Successfully married retired couples we have interviewed care deeply about each other's health. Their advice—plan an exercise program together. Eat lots of fruits and vegetables.

Take your medicine(s) as prescribed. Take your vitamins. Keep your weight under control. You see, healthy people live longer. And isn't it comforting to know that you did everything you could to add to those years together and to improve the quality of each other's lives.

7. ***Manage your finances together once retirement occurs.*** The worst thing that can happen according to one of the couples we interviewed is to "outlive your money!" Frankly, life has no guarantees so the best strategy is to manage your resources together, often with the help of a professional financial planner, and with the assumption you will live longer than you might anticipate in an actuarial sense. Our successfully married retired couples have told us repeatedly that they cannot emphasize enough the importance of working together to manage your finances in retirement.

Reinvesting your time in the one you love can bring enormous benefits. In retirement, the simple things still matter.

Until Death Do Us Part

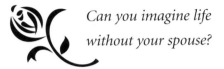

*Can you imagine life
without your spouse?*

AT THE END OF EACH INTERVIEW we conduct with happily and successfully married couples we ask the most powerful question of our interview protocol—"Can you imagine life without your spouse?" The question always draws tears to the eyes of the couple we are interviewing. We have asked them a question they have repressed. It is a question no loving couple wants to think about. The answer is, however, nearly always the same—"No!"

When we take our marriage vows—"until death do us part"— we never imagine that some day it will all come to an end. But all marriages and relationships do end, of that you can be sure. So, how do we prepare for it?

Our advice is, never dwell on or contemplate the question. It doesn't matter. What is important is that we love our spouse, that we enjoy our spouse, and that we live our life with them to the fullest. If you think about the inevitable, your relationship will end in a different way. Yes, a different way.

Here is how it works. If you spend your time imagining the end you will never do all of the things required to deal with the beginning and the middle. You will lose the richness and beauty of each moment. You will, in the end, misplace the essence of your relationship with each other. Your relationship will be based on the end instead of the possibilities.

When you cannot imagine life without the one you love, you have reached the "nirvana" of your loving and committed relationship. But to dwell on the inevitable end of your life together diminishes the here and now and spoils all the joy that lies ahead.

REFLECTIONS ON MARRIAGE

IN MARRIAGE SIMPLE THINGS MATTER

Reflections on a
Half-Century of Marriage

*Being in love and being loved is a
great way to spend your life.*

WE JUST CELEBRATED OUR
52nd Wedding Anniversary. Just imagine, being successfully
married for 52 years! And as a friend of ours used to say, "And to
the same person!" Having a successful marriage is certainly a
worthy life goal. We are one of those fortunate couples that got to
celebrate our golden anniversary.

While we spend a lot of time studying and writing about the
successful long-term relationships of others, we decided to spend
some time today thinking about our own wonderful marriage that
has spanned more than five decades of our lives.

One of our favorite lines from a song says it all—"Still crazy after
all these years." That's the way we feel about each other—still crazy
in love after all these years.

Fifty-three years ago, a small town Missouri boy met a California
girl at College. His friends were the sons and daughters of Missouri
farmers and other good folks who worked on the railroad. Her
friends were California surfers and swimmers. She was bronze
colored, tall, and had that look of a long-distance swimmer. It was
fun for Charley to see her walking down the sidewalk, grooving to

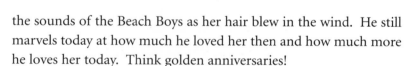

the sounds of the Beach Boys as her hair blew in the wind. He still marvels today at how much he loved her then and how much more he loves her today. Think golden anniversaries!

Liz used to listen for hours while Charley sang Elvis songs to her. She once said, "Gosh, you really do sound like him!" Charley turned red, but he was proud. Elvis was his hero. And now Liz was!

Liz tells Charley every day how much she loves him and how she couldn't imagine life without him. Charley smiles, then cries. It feels so good to be loved so much. He reflects on his life with Liz and wonders how he got so lucky. He loves to tell everyone within earshot how he "married up!" He swears that most men do. Liz says she feels the same way about him. Hmmmm . . . maybe we both married up!

It's always fun for us to reflect on life together. We have so many common interests. We are alike in many ways. But through it all we have maintained our individuality and our respective identities— with enormous respect for our differences as well as our similarities.

Helping others build loving relationships that last a lifetime has become one of our greatest goals in life. Being in love and being loved is a great way to spend your life. And while we truly and sincerely believe that successful loving relationships are not all that difficult to understand and make work, we continue to be surprised by the fact that so many "people in love" won't do the simple things required to make their love last.

On the occasion of our 52nd wedding anniversary we renewed our commitment to help others learn the important lessons about love and relationships so that they can practice the simple truths about love everyday of their lives together.

May your love be as strong as ours and your commitment to make your love work even stronger. Go be happy and in love. There is nothing like it.

Two Lovebirds Who
Found Lasting Love

*There is much to learn from
these two lovebirds who have
found "Lasting Love."*

*L*ASTING LOVE, 'til death do us part. Married couples repeat this stanza or some variation of it in most marriage ceremonies. In its essence, two people commit to each other their love, their faithfulness, and their sacred honor for the rest of their lives. Many times, it works out just that way. Other times, the promise falls short. But in the case of Sandy and Pris, was sustained for a lifetime.

Of all the interviews we have conducted throughout the USA and around the world, no love seemed greater than the love between Sandy and Pris. These two are a perfect example of what it means to find lasting love.

We interviewed them in their home several years ago. Sandy had retired as CEO of a large American corporation. He invested his time and money in philanthropic causes across the USA, particularly in character education. Pris was interested in the arts and was a big supporter of opera theatre, in particular. Their passion for their philanthropic causes was amazing and their commitment to their work was heartwarming. If you ever wanted to spend an evening with two of the most generous, endearing, enchanting, and wonderful people you could meet, these are the two that you would want to be with.

Before we interviewed Sandy and Pris, we thought we knew a lot about love and relationships. That evening, however, we got an education for which we will be eternally grateful.

Sandy loved Pris absolutely and completely. He loved her without conditions. He loved her since the first time he saw her on the ski slopes near Santa Fe, New Mexico. During our interview, he looked at his bride of over 60 years and said, "She is still the same beautiful woman I married so many years ago!" He had tears in his eyes when he spoke those words. Pris choked back the tears, as she looked deep into his eyes. These were the faces of love.

Pris responded that she fell in love with this handsome, dashing man with his white skis as soon as she saw him glide effortlessly down the snow-covered mountain.

Sandy and Pris loved each other from the bottom of their respective hearts and often said, "We have been married for more than 60 years and are more in love now than ever." Everything they said to us during the interview reinforced their unqualified love for each other.

There were many lessons we learned from Sandy and Pris. We want to share with you what they believe to be the most important.

First, they shared a mutual admiration society. They always supported and encouraged each other.

Secondly, they loved each other very much and said so many times during each day of their lives together.

Thirdly, they were totally honest with each other. They showed integrity in their interactions, had undying trust in each other, and demonstrated their character by their words and by their actions.

And finally, their most important lesson of all—"Never go to bed mad at each other."

Sandy and Pris had great admiration and respect for each other. It showed in their words, their actions, their expressions, and in Sandy's case, in his voice as he sang love songs to her every morning—off key sometimes, but always full of love and emotion.

As we concluded our interview with our usual question, "Can you imagine life without each other?" we got the answer we expected, but not a word was spoken. Their eyes welted up with tears, they gazed lovingly at each other for an extended period of time, and then they looked at us and smiled. No words were necessary. We knew their answer as well as we knew our own—lasting love 'til death do us part.

We know you will agree—Sandy and Pris are an inspiration to everyone. Their wonderful 60+ years of marriage attest to the power of their relationship and the depth of their love. There is much to learn from these two lovebirds who found "Lasting Love."

Sandy passed away first, and Pris joined him in eternity a few years later. Their love story ended on Earth, but we have no doubt it has continued in the great beyond.

You Can Learn a Lot
About Love by Dancing

*There is something
magical about dancing.*

*T*ODAY WE WERE TOLD
a delightful story about life and love, and dancing. The story was apparently reported on the CBS Evening News and shared with us by a colleague. We heard a similar story a few months ago during a conversation with a couple we were interviewing. We will change the names in our story to protect the innocent. And you'll see why.

It seems that Mary was married to Ned for 50 years. They celebrated their Golden Anniversary together. Mary loved Ned and Ned loved Mary. It was a marriage success story. And while their marriage was a happy one, it had a tragic ending—Ned died.

Ned's death for a couple married for 50 years is probably not all that unusual or unexpected. At his death, Ned was 88 and Mary was 85. The sad truth is, people die. And often times the one you love deeply, dies. It is part of the cycle of life. Sad, but true.

But this story has a twist to it. You see, as committed as Mary was to Ned and as much as she loved him, her life with Ned for all those many years left her with an unaddressed beef about him. He didn't fulfill all her needs.

You see, Mary loves to dance. It was and has been her passion for most of her life. She reports that she dreamed about her "Knight in dancing armor" for most of her life. She would find her dancing man and they would dance the night away. You have heard about the "golden slipper" at the ball (a dance), well, this was a story about the dancing shoes.

When she married Ned, she soon discovered that he was not a dancer at all. In fact, he didn't dance with her during their 50 years of marriage! Not once. She never went dancing. Again, a sad story, but true.

But this story has a dancing twist. When Ned died, Mary met a new man. We shall call him George. George had a passion for dancing. And when they met at a dance hall in Oklahoma, it was love at *first dance.*

Mary had found her dancing man after all these years. And dance they did. They danced and danced and danced and danced!

There is something magical about dancing. As our Texas friend says, "You can learn a lot about love by dancing." The case of Mary and Ned, and now the dancing man, George, illustrates his point very well we think.

Now the story gets really interesting. According to Mary, her new man is a dancing king. George loves Mary and Mary loves George. Through their dancing, Mary at 88 and George at 83, are considering getting married. Dancing has done it again! George and Mary are getting ready to Tango!

Here's the "dancing" twist to this story—Mary and George have been living together for nearly a year now—and they are **not** married. George says they were taught better, but at their age, "What's the rush? We will get married soon enough!" When you are in your late 80's, we call that great optimism! Life and love— saved by dancing!

The next time you are feeling down and blue, and out of love, just remember the story of Mary and George. Life and love can begin again when you are in your 80's. Love can begin again after you have enjoyed your Golden Anniversary with someone you loved for so many years who leaves you through death.

Sometimes those we love die. Sometimes a marriage ends for no reason other than death. But always remember this—true love can be found again. Your new dancing partner can be just around the next twirl at the local dance club!

Go dancing tonight. You never know.

Traditional Marriage Is Alive and Well

Marriage is alive and well in the USA and around the world. To suggest otherwise is to ignore the real facts.

*W*E KNOW, WE HEAR THEM all the time—those purveyors of half-truths, un-truths, and political agendas. You know the ones—the ones who continually pronounce to the world that traditional marriage is dead. Well, all we can say is—don't believe it!

Statistically there is substantial support for our point of view. According to the best estimates we can find, there were some 45 million marriages worldwide last year. There were some 9 million divorces in the same year. If you do the math you can see that worldwide, marriages outnumber divorces by a ratio of 5 to 1. Stated clearly and succinctly, there were five marriages for every one divorce in the world last year. Hardly sounds like the death of marriage to us.

The truth is—based on the facts—marriage is alive and well in the world today. There is no disputing these facts. So, why do the purveyors of negativism continue to distort the truth? Why do certain members of the media and so many of those who write books about the demise of marriage continue to distort the reality of what is?

There are probably lots of reasons to explain this phenomenon. Foremost among them are the polltakers. Polltakers are notorious for asking the wrong questions or asking poorly phrased questions, and then reporting results that are, well, grossly out of touch with the reality they purport to represent.

Here is a recent example. A Zogby Poll got much national attention a few years ago. One of their so-called "findings" was the following: "Issues related to trust in relationships vary significantly among different generations. Younger respondents are more likely to want the truth from their partner, even if it hurts - more than 85% of respondents in their 20s said they always want the truth, compared to 79% of those in their 50s and 60s."

We wonder, did it ever occur to the pollsters that there is a "maturity factor" at work here? Did they ever consider that younger respondents "want the truth" from their partner "even if it hurts" is simply the admonitions of naïve young people who don't yet understand that "sometimes the truth hurts." Older folks have gained great wisdom over the years and they know that sometimes "words hurt." Words sometimes have unintended consequences. Older and wiser people understand this. Older folks tend to be more careful with what they express, especially if their words might have negative consequences.

And one more point about this poll—did anyone ask if the difference between 85% (the percentage of young people who want the truth) and 79% of older adults who always "want the truth" was statistically significant? In every poll, there is an error of measurement. True differences occur outside of this error range. In other words, is the 6% difference reported by the pollster really meaningful?

We offer the aforementioned example to demonstrate that the questions asked and to whom, often determines the answer received. But, the answer received is not always the answer that is the most honest portrayal of the truth or the reality of it all.

Here is another example. A recent *New York Times* article reported that fewer than half of American women were now married. Yet, they included in their population of "un-married women" girls who were 15, 16, and 17 years old and women whose husbands were deceased! See our point? Does anyone really believe that 15-year-old girls are "women?" Of course not! Does anyone really believe that a 70-year-old widow is "unmarried?" Of course not!

So, here is where we are. Marriage is alive and well in the world today! It is still among the greatest contribution to social order that exists in the world today. Marriage is not in danger just because a pollster asks a question that suggests it is. Marriage is not in danger just because people who report statistical data report it incorrectly or in a way that leads to a false conclusion about marriage.

The truth is, marriage is alive and well worldwide AND in the United States of America. Marriage is still the greatest and most profound commitment to love that exists, irrespective of the so-called truths exposed by pollsters who might suggest something otherwise based on faulty or distorted polling data.

When you discount for the number of divorcees in America who get divorced multiple times, the "divorce rate" and its impact is much less than that reported by the popular media. As we have said before, the "real" divorce rate in the USA in terms of its true societal impact is far less than the 50% rate reported. When discounted for those who have multiple divorces, the "true" impact divorce rate is probably closer to 35% or 40%.

As researchers for over 37 years, all we ask is that the good folks who read polls and crunch numbers do so very carefully. The conclusions you draw will often be different from those concluded by the pollsters, the popular media, and the so-called experts.

Marriage is alive and well in the USA and around the world. To suggest otherwise is to ignore the real facts.

Love and Marriage in France

The greatest romantic country in the world –
and a very secular country as well –
is getting interested in marriage again.

RECENTLY, WE AGAIN TRAVELED to Europe to conduct more interviews with successfully married couples for our next book entitled, *Love and Marriage in Romantic Countries.* Since we had not been to France in several of years, we were beginning to believe the media reports about how the French did not like Americans. So, we braced ourselves for the difficulties we might encounter as two American authors and researchers asking intimate questions about love and marriage in France. Our fears and the media reports could not have been further from the truth.

First of all, the French people were delightful! They were wonderfully warm, open, friendly and courteous beyond imagination. Everywhere we went they treated us like members of their family. From the hotels we stayed in to the local bistros, the people were marvelous. On buses, trains, subways, and in cabs, we were greeted with open arms and great warmth.

And while we have heard for years the notion that "French people will be more friendly if you speak to them in French," we found that a warm handshake and a big smile spoke volumes in French! They were polite to us and we reciprocated. We struggled with each other's languages but we managed. Big smiles, hand signs, and hugs go a long way in most of the foreign countries we have visited. That's for sure.

Our travels took us throughout France, with a focus on Paris and Lyon—both wonderful cities with fabulous cuisine, great wine, sights to behold, and history to tell. But more than anything, with all the amenities of these two great cities, we were struck by the friendliness and warmth of the French people. We were there for nearly two weeks and only have splendid experiences to report. The French passion for food, wine, life and romance cannot be missed if you just strike up a conversation with someone, observe couples strolling down the Champs Elysee, or when you mingle in a small café or bistro.

And the couples we interviewed were marvelous, which brings us to the main point of our story. You have probably heard that the French are no longer interested in marriage or some variation on that theme. Don't you believe it! The couples we interviewed who had been successfully and happily married for 30 to 77 years reported great satisfaction in their marriage and would do it all over again. But here is where it gets interesting—we found the same themes in young French couples that were in love. The ones we interviewed loved each other very much and were looking forward to getting married, just like their aunts and uncles, parents, and grand parents before them. In fact, the word on the French streets is that marriage is making a very nice comeback in France! We heard nothing while we were there to dispute that notion.

Isn't that wonderful news! The greatest romantic country in the world—and a very secular country as well—is getting interested in marriage again. That is encouraging news, indeed.

When we summarized our recent interview data from France we were struck by how similar the characteristics that defined their successful marriages and relationships were to those in the USA. They were virtually identical. It seems that successful marriages around the world or in romantic countries have common themes. Frankly, we continue to be extremely excited about our findings.

Prior to this visit some of the countries where we had already interviewed couples over the years are Argentina, Australia, Austria, Belgium, Brazil, Canada, Chile, China, Denmark, France, Germany, Great Britain, Greece, Italy, Luxembourg, Mexico, Monaco, Norway, Portugal, Spain, Sweden, Switzerland, Taiwan, The Philippines and The Netherlands. On our most recent trip we interviewed additional couples in Belgium, Great Britain, France, and Luxembourg. Next we are off to South Africa to interview couples with successful marriages of more than 30 years.

While we have enjoyed immensely the couples we have interviewed in all of the countries we have visited, we particularly enjoyed our recent interviews with French couples. There are a multitude of reasons why. But if you pushed us to name just one, it would have to be their passion for enjoying the romance of life and their love for each other. We do not ever remember feeling so comfortable and welcomed by the people of a foreign country than we did in our recent trip to France.

As we began to write the individual and collective stories of these engaging French couples with successful marriages for our next book, we found ourselves wanting to share some of those findings with you now. We were just too excited to wait!

The Look of Love Is
Alive and Well in Brazil

One of the endearing
characteristics of life in Brazil
is the focus on the family.

*I*N RIO DE JANEIRO WE SAW the look of love from two lovebirds who have been in love since they were eight years old.

We had the great pleasure of interviewing Attilio Borriello and his bride of 51 years, Arlette. And trust us when we say this—they look like love! They are the look of love.

Attilio and Arlette are from San Lorenzo, Minas Gerais, Brazil, the third largest metropolitan area of the country and about a four-hour drive from Rio. They were in Rio visiting family, and we were introduced to them by their 23-year-old granddaughter, Cristiana.

We were blessed by the opportunity to interview them today over lunch at A Garota de Ipanema (*The Girl from Ipanema*) restaurant. Let us say up front, Attilio and Arlette are a near perfect match for the profile of successful marriage we have found in our travels around the world. In fact, their marital relationship of nearly 52 years is a mirror image of the long-time, successfully married couples we have interviewed over the years. They are what love is!

Over their 51 years of marriage they have birthed three children and are the proud grandparents of six grandchildren. They speak often and adoringly of their extended family.

In fact, one of the endearing characteristics of life in Brazil is the focus on the family. Many have told us that the principle reason the divorce rate in Brazil is only 20% is because of the strength of the family. Divorce is certainly allowable in Brazil, but with the loving support of the extended family, it is not the choice of first resort for most Brazilians, as it often is for many who live in the USA.

But as in all marriages, the most important determiner of success and longevity is the relationship between husband and wife. That relationship, in the end, trumps everything else. In the case of Attilio and Arlette, their relationship is amongst the most loving and supportive relationships we have ever witnessed. Our interview with them reinforced everything we have learned about successful marriage over the years.

In a nutshell, here is what makes their marriage work so well:

First and foremost they love each other deeply. You can see it in their eyes. You can see it in the way they lovingly and adoringly gazed at each other during the course of our interview with them. And you could see it in the way their eyes teared up when we asked what we have come to believe is the most important and telling question about the best marriages—"Can you imagine life without each other?" Their answer to this question was an emphatic "No!" Attilio went on to report that he "Doesn't ever want to think about it!" To these two lovebirds "death do us part" is the only way their marriage on Earth will ever end. They have committed their lives, their love, and their sacred honor until the end of time.

Secondly, Attilio and Arlette, learned early on in their relationship that to disagree from time to time is natural, even in the best marriages, but to escalate the disagreements into heated arguments is to be avoided at all costs. They have mastered the art of compromise. They have learned that a raised voice only exacerbates their occasional disagreement over an issue. Arlette reported that they both have learned to back away when they disagree over something and come back to the discussion later when the emotion of the moment has dissipated. Wonderful advice, don't you think?

And there is no question about it—Attilio and Arlette are best friends! They were friends long before they got married and have sustained that friendship throughout their marriage.

When asked to describe his friend, Arlette, Attilio used words like, "wonder woman," "my wonderful friend," "the best woman in the world," and "a strong person." Arlette described Attilio as her "best friend," "her hero," "her lover," "her everything!" The endearing terms about their friendship flowed from their lips. Their friendship is truly, "A Beautiful Love Story," the name they reported to us they would give to a book written about their enduring marriage.

Truth is, there is so much we could write about our new friends. There is so much we could say about them and their love for each other. But for now, we will summarize what they believe to be the most important reasons for the amazing success of their marriage over the years beyond the previously stated reasons.

Share and do many things together; always try to look your best for each other; be respectful of each other unfailingly; endeavor to interject variety and spice into your relationship; help each other to stay healthy (the right foods, annual physical exams, properly taking medications, etc.); share life's burdens; remember the special moments together; talk about anything and everything with your spouse; and above all else, touch each other often during each and every day. We would call this advice, advice to live by!

One final note to share—when Attilio and Arlette celebrated their 50th Wedding Anniversary (their Golden Anniversary) their family gave them a big celebration party at the JW Marriott Hotel on Copacabana Beach in Rio de Janeiro. Their room number was 714. Our room for our stay in Rio was 714! In addition, their granddaughter, Cristiana, works at the Marriott and checked us in and arranged for our interview with her grandparents. And the parallels continue – our daughter's name is Kristina. We think there is a good omen in there somewhere!

A Portrait of Love and Marriage in the Caribbean

These two lovebirds broke the trend many years ago and are a living portrait of love and marriage, Caribbean style.

HERE WE SIT GAZING AT the beautiful turquoise blue ocean from our perch on the balcony of our room at the Marriott Casa Magna in Cancun, Quintana Roo, Mexico. We are conducting interviews with successfully married couples in Mexico as we continue our travels around the world searching for the best marriages.

Today we had the pleasure of interviewing Isabel and Luis, two lovebirds who have been married for 33 years. They come from very different backgrounds but are very much in love with each other.

Luis grew up terribly poor in a small town in Mexico just to the west, Leona Vicario. While his beginnings were humble, he has done well for himself and his family over the years. He has recently become the general manager for a resort hotel in the Caribbean, no small accomplishments for a boy who grew up with 10 siblings in a wooden pole hut with a dirt floor and a palm leaf thatched roof.

Most of us can only imagine what it was like to grow up that poor in a community where there is very little opportunity. Luis cut wood stakes at an early age and sold them to other families to burn for cooking and for keeping their homes warm at night. We were so curious about the little town he grew up in that we rented a car and drove to it earlier this week. It doesn't look like much has changed over the years. And those thatched palm leave roofs still adorn the modest huts with the dirt floors for many of the village residents. Luis has, indeed, come a long way.

Isabel had a different upbringing. Her father would be considered rich by most any standard. The view from her bedroom growing up was the beautiful turquoise colored ocean of the Caribbean Sea near Playa del Carmen, Quintana Roo, Mexico. Her father was a land developer along the Mexican Riviera by the Caribbean Ocean. He got in on the ground floor of a series of resorts that now dot the white sands of the Caribbean Ocean from Cancun to Tulum. Tourism is now the number one industry in this part of Mexico and Isabel's father got very rich developing those luxury resorts.

As you can imagine, the first time Luis and Isabel met they paid little attention to each other beyond a nod of the head when a friend of one of her brothers, Artemio, introduced them at a local Mercado one Saturday afternoon in Playa del Carmen, where Isabel shopped and Luis worked at a local hotel washing dishes.

Over time, this daughter of a wealthy land developer and this son of a pauper began to cross paths more frequently at various locations around town. And as curious as it might sound, they began, as Luis says, "making eyes at each other!" One warm Caribbean afternoon Luis asked this beautiful rich girl if she would go out with him and for some unexplainable reason according to Luis, she said yes!

Given the traditions of the time, Isabel's father would certainly object strenuously if he found out his daughter was dating a dishwasher. In her father's day, the families of the bride and groom arranged the marriage. The thought of a rich girl marrying a poor man was simply out of the question! Luis and Isabel knew that, but their love for each other grew every time they were together and grew even stronger when they were apart.

So you are asking yourself, "What is the rest of this story?" Did love triumph over family traditions? Did Luis marry Isabel over the objections of her father? Well, the truth is, Isabel's father loved her deeply and while he had great apprehension about her daughter's choice of a poor dishwasher for a husband, he did see great promise in Luis. In fact, he was quite impressed with Luis' intelligence and industriousness.

More importantly, he trusted and respected his daughter's judgment and as he frequently said, his daughter "was just like his wife"—strong, independent, a mind of her own—and he admired his daughter for being the same! In a country where men often ruled the roost after marriage, Isabel's father was a non-traditional-ist. He admired strong women and could not stand in the way of his daughter's desires when it came to the man in her life. Luis was a good, decent, and honorable young man and if his daughter wanted to marry him, that was good enough for her father.

The wedding was lovely and for a marriage between rich and poor, it was a marriage to remember. The guest list was long and represented all the social classes of Mexico. The rich and famous met the poor and the underprivileged. And in the end, they all danced the night away to the sounds of the best mariachi band in Playa del Carmen! It seems that in the end, people are just people, irrespective of their socio-economic class. The marriage of Luis and Isabel is a testament to that.

Now, 33 years later, Luis and Isabel are still madly in love. They have succeeded where most similar cross-social class marriages in Mexico have failed. Their marriage has taught them much about the power of love, the importance of family, and the lessons of strength and conviction. These two lovebirds broke the trend many years ago and are a living portrait of love and marriage, Caribbean style.

Simple things matter in love and marriage. Choosing the one you love for love tops the list.

We'd Marry Each Other
All Over Again!

And when all is said and done,
you will say,
"I would do it all over again.

A FEW YEARS AGO IN PROVIDENCE, Rhode Island, 300 married couples said, "I do," all over again. Isn't that wonderful! The participating couples were married from 25 to 70 years and loved each other so much that they chose to reaffirm their commitment to each other by renewing their marriage vows, and in a very public way. They promised once more, "To have and to hold, from this day forward, for better, for worse, for richer, for poorer, in sickness or in health, to love and to cherish 'til death do us part."

This "good news" story caught our attention when we saw a video clip on one of the nightly news shows about it. It struck a chord with us because for nearly four decades we have interviewed successfully married couples that were married between 30 and 77 years.

One of the questions in our interview protocol asks the couple we are interviewing if they would marry each other all over again. The answer tells you a lot about the quality of their relationship and the success of their marriage, and it provides a true testament to their love for each other.

With the happily married couples, the answer is nearly always a resounding, "yes!" On the other hand, for those that equivocate, you get a sense that all is not well with their relationship. The successfully married couples we have interviewed over the years gave their lives, their love, and their sacred honor to each other and would not hesitate to make that same commitment again.

You see, true love *is* forever. We know that skeptics abound when it comes to this notion, but many of them miss the most important point of its meaning. Let us explain.

When people fall in love do they say, "I will fall in love with you until somebody else comes along I love more." Do they say, "You are the love of my life today, but I will look for a new one tomorrow." Worse yet, just imagine someone setting a time limit on their love— "I will love you for ten years and then will move on to another lover." Sounds silly when you think about it, huh?

Why commit your love to someone if you don't think it will last forever? True love, it seems to us, is all about commitment. You can't truly love someone if you do not believe your relationship to be permanent. If you feel that it is not, what you are feeling is probably not real love but infatuation or some other emotion that disguises itself as love.

When you truly know you are in love, you are ready to make the commitment to another person. But that is only half the story—the other person has to feel that way as well. It does, as we often say, take two to Tango!

We have learned many lessons over the years about lasting love. Long-lasting and successful relationships begin and end with unqualified and undying love and commitment. To think otherwise is to set yourself up for failure in love, and life.

May the love of your life share their life with you until the end. And when all is said and done, you will say, "I would do it all over again."

Here's to lasting love.

EPILOG

IN MARRIAGE SIMPLE THINGS MATTER

Some Marriages Are Not Worth Saving

The simple truth is, some marriages and relationships should not and cannot be saved.

*W*E HAVE SAID FOR MANY years, "Most marriages and relationships can be saved, but not all!" And our corollary has always been—"Most marriages and relationships are worth saving, but not all!" Here's what we mean.

In the case of abuse—sexual, physical, mental—many failing marriages and relationships are simply not worth saving. In fact, to attempt to save them puts one or both partners in the relationship at risk for further abuse.

Frankly, we know that some marriages and relationships are not worth saving. And do you know how hard this statement is to make for people like us—the eternal optimists who always see a pot of gold at the end of the rainbow—who always see a silver lining? Unfortunately, the truth is the truth when it comes to love and life . . . and marriage.

Our seven decades of life and nearly four decades of research on the topics of love and marriage, tell us that some relationships become so poisoned, so dysfunctional, and so hopeless, that it is better to end them than to operate under the illusion that they are worth saving or can be saved.

We recently interviewed a young American couple that had been married for 14 years. It was clear from the beginning of our interview with them that this was not a match made in heaven. In fact, this marriage had failed so miserably that the only just and decent thing to do was end it. End it now! No amount of counseling and therapy, no amount of praying, and no amount of hoping were going to save this marriage.

For 14 years, the husband had "mentally abused" his wife. He discounted her every word. He made her feel insignificant by his words, his deeds, and by his actions. And even though his wife was pursuing a doctoral degree at one of America's most prestigious universities, he treated her like she was some kind of dumb cluck—someone capable of nothing significant, lasting, or meaningful.

When we interviewed them, it became clear to us that she had had enough. She had had enough of his disrespect, his belittling, his mental abuse, and his coldness. She had finally decided that if she were to have any life at all, their marriage and their relationship would have to become history. So, she decided to end it.

The truth is, the mental anguish she suffered over the years had taken its toll—on her, her three children, and on her marital relationship. She asked us the most profound question of all—"How can I continue to live with a man that makes me feel so worthless, so insignificant, and so meaningless. How can I continue to live with a man that respects me so little?"

Her questions reveal the truth of all this. Sometimes it is just time to move on. Sometimes, to save your soul you have to free yourself of all that is oppressive. Sometimes, you must remove the albatross around your neck if you have any hope of living out your life with happiness, hope, self-respect, and meaningfulness.

Sometimes, you simply must move on with your life before it is too late. For the couple we interviewed, her time had come. The action she must take was clear. The action she must take to save her soul and the souls of her three children became clear to her—if she had any hope at all for her life and her children's lives, the time to move on was now!

The simple truth is, some marriages and relationships should not and cannot be saved. As harsh and evident as this truth is, it cannot be avoided in the case of some marriages and relationships. And in the end, when you have exhausted the solutions available to you, you simply must cut the tithes that bind.

For more than 37 years now, we have interviewed couples around the world and across cultures and continents. Most of the time we have concluded that most marriages and relationships can and should be saved—but not all! When you can look in the mirror and honestly and truthfully say that you did your best to save your relationship with another human being, but to no avail, then ending it is the right thing to do. Life is too short to waste it in torment, in abuse, and in lost love.

Sometimes, it is time to move on.

Special Thanks

*W*HEN YOU ENGAGE IN A "labor of love" for more than 37 years, there are a lot of people to thank, especially when your work culminates in a finished book like *In Marriage Simple Things Matter.* We have worked with many wonderful people along the way, but several stand out.

First and foremost, we would like to thank all of those marvelous and wonderful couples we have interviewed over the years. We have learned so much from them about love, successful marriage, and relationships. They were and continue to be an inspiration for us, and a model for successful marriage in the USA and around the world.

In addition, we owe a huge debt of gratitude to the wonderful folks at both Walsworth and Briarcliff Publishing companies. They have stood beside us over the years and took us on when others doubted the importance of our work. All we ever wanted to do with our books was promote the positive benefits of successful marriage. They believed in our "successful marriage projects" and we will be forever indebted to them for their support.

And to our friends at the world renowned Gallup Organization, we want to thank you for teaching us to understand that if you want to know something about success, study success. We have followed your advice over the years and thank you for your support from the bottom of our collective hearts.

Finally, we have been lovebirds for some 53 years. We believe in each other and in ourselves. Nearly 52 years of successful marriage is a testament to our enduring love for each other.

Our Wonder Dog Louie

Where Our Marriage Began

IN MARRIAGE SIMPLE THINGS MATTER

My Reflections
on Love and Marriage